FATE, LOVE, AND ECSTASY

Fate, Love, and Ecstasy

Wisdom from the Lesser-Known Goddesses of the Greeks

JOHN A. SANFORD

CHIRON PUBLICATIONS · WILMETTE, ILLINOIS

Permissions
Jacket: Painting *Three Graces* by mykulanjelo, fine artist and illustrator working in Wales, Wisconsin. Copyright © 1993 by mykulanjelo. Reproduction by permission of the artist.

Library of Congress Catalog Card Number: 95–14099

Printed in the United States of America.
Copyedited by Andrew C. Baker.
Book design by Vivian Bradbury.
Jacket design by D. J. Hyde.

Library of Congress Cataloging-in-Publication Data:

Sanford, John A.
    Fate, love, and ecstasy : wisdom from the lesser-known goddesses of the Greeks / John A. Sanford.
        p.   cm.
    Includes bibliographical references and index.
    ISBN 0–933029–96–9
    1. Goddesses, Greek.   2. Spiritual life.   I. Title.
BL795.G63S26   1995
292.2'114—dc20   95–14099
                                                                              CIP

ISBN 0–933029–96–9

To my father,

Edgar L. Sanford II,

whose library of ancient Greek books and texts
first aroused my interest in the Greek language and spirit,
and whose Greek lexicon I continue to use today.

CONTENTS

A Note on the Text

In this book, references to the Bible are to the Revised Standard Version. References to classical literature are to the Loeb Classical Library editions published by Heinemann and the Harvard University Press. The Loeb/Heinemann bilingual editions are readily available in most libraries, and since section and line numbering is consistent among different translations of classical Greek and Latin texts, citations are given by line number (and by chapter and volume number where necessary), so that readers may examine these texts for themselves if they wish. All references to classical Greek tragedies are to line numbers. The reader will find a list of all these sources, and other scholarly works cited, appended to the text.

INTRODUCTION

The Hunt for the Purple Fish and the Lesser-Known Goddesses of the Greeks

One day, while I was exploring some of the mysteries of the Greek language in one of my Greek–English lexicons, my eye fell by chance upon a word hitherto unknown to me, a word which had such a peculiar meaning that it reached out, as it were, and grasped my attention. In fact, the word had two meanings, not unusual in Greek except that in this case the meanings seemed unrelated. The first meaning given for this word in my lexicon was "to search for the purple fish." The second meaning was "to search in the depths of one's mind."[1] What mystery was this? Why should a fish be called "the purple fish"? And what did this have to do with searching in the depths of one's mind?

It took some work, but I finally unearthed the solution to the mystery. The word in question was the Greek word *kalchainō*. The word *kalchē* is Greek for purple. The word *kalchainō* means roughly "to search for the purple." It seems that in antiquity the Greeks extracted a fine purple dye from a mollusk which could be found at the bottom of the sea, around the islands which abound in the waters of Greece. The hunt for this "purple fish" was done by divers, who often descended to great depths to

1

find and bring to the surface the valuable mollusks from which the fine purple dye was made.

Now, the Greek language abounds in images, which makes it psychologically rich. When the Greeks thought of diving into the sea to retrieve the valuable prize of the purple shellfish, they associated this action with diving into the depths of themselves, to bring to the surface of their minds the valuable treasures of their inner life.

This inner "sea" that the ancient Greeks were wont to explore is what we would today call the "collective unconscious"; in fact, the collective unconscious often appears in our dreams as the ocean, or some other extensive body of water. In general, the unconscious refers to everything pertaining to or belonging to our personality of which we are ordinarily unaware. Those elements of our personality which are derived from our personal past life-experience, but which have been forgotten or repressed, constitute the "personal unconscious." But there is also within us something like the repository of the "memories" of the whole human race. Carl Jung called this unconscious realm within us the "collective unconscious," because it is shared alike by all human beings. The principal contents of the collective unconscious are the "archetypes," those primordial, living psychic patterns within us which both evoke psychic energy, and shape it according to the forms peculiar to that particular archetype.

All of life's important and oft-repeated experiences have their archetypes in the collective unconscious. When a situation in life is ripe for a particular archetype to be made manifest, then the energy-system of the appropriate archetype is constellated, and made available to the ego in such a forcible way that the archetype may rule or dominate a great deal of the ego's life. Thus, there is an archetype for love, for war, for life, for death, for being a mother or a father, for the child, for illness, for healing, for dying, for meeting, for saying goodbye. On and on goes the list of life's great experiences, which have been repeated over and over again in human beings, many hundreds of millions of times, since the dawn of human life; and, for each such experience, there is an archetype.

It is the viewpoint of Jungian psychology that behind the myths which we find all over the world exist these archetypes of the collective unconscious; therefore, myths are "archetypal," that is, they express in their own way the living unconscious patterns within the human psyche that shape our lives and destinies. The archetypes are personified and exemplified in mythology, because the archetypes naturally present themselves to consciousness in the form of imagination. Everything—from seemingly chance fantasies to epic and dramatic stories and creations—has its roots in the imaginative quality of the archetypal world. This is why Jung's psychology finds in myths a treasure-house of meaning, for myths contain vital elements of our interior psychological and spiritual life. They are, like dreams, the "royal road" to the unconscious.

One would think that this approach to mythology would be valued in our world today; and so it is by those who are conversant with and open to the idea of the archetypes. Many psychologists, however, repudiate ideas of the archetypes and the collective unconscious, dismissing these ideas as mere mysticism. Unfortunately, this attitude, rooted as it is in a narrow rationalism and materialism, prevents people from accessing the deeper strata of their psyches. Most mythologists, similarly, appear equally opposed to Jung's approach, perhaps because accepting his theory would require them to revise considerably their previous estimates of the origins and meaning of myth. One of the most recent books on the origin of mythology, *Approaches to Greek Mythology*, summarizes seven current theories of the origin of mythology, including a chapter on psychoanalytic theory, but does not even mention Jung's name (Edmunds 1990).

One objection made to Jung's idea of the archetypes as the source for ancient mythologies, with their pantheons of gods and goddesses, is that this idea "puts God into the soul and locks him up there."[2] This choice of language—locked up in the soul, as though it were a prison—reveals the modern prejudice against the soul. For this soul of ours is no prison, but is a vast inner psychic realm which, though it exists as a psychic entity within ourselves, has contact with everything else in life that partakes of the nature of soul. The psychic realm in which the archetypes exist is, therefore, no prison; a prison is by definition narrow, confined and limited, while the world of the soul,

3

though the smallest of the small, is also as deep as the ocean and as vast as the sky.

For this reason, mystics and seers the world over have seen the soul as the abiding place of God. For the early Christian, the divine Logos of God lived in the soul, for which reason the early Christian philosopher and theologian Tertullian once declared, "From the beginning the knowledge of God is the dowry of the soul, one and the same amongst the Egyptians, and the Syrians, and the tribes of Pontus" (Tertullian 1957, 278). This was also true for the ancient Greeks, so much so that Plato once declared, "After the gods the soul is most divine" (Plato 1984b, 726). And the Greek playwright Aeschylus could say, "The divine power still abides even in the soul of one enslaved."[3]

Thanks to Jung's theory of the archetypes, mythology may be rescued from the scrap heap onto which modern rationalistic attitudes have cast it. Myths need no longer be regarded merely as quaint stories which children might like but which cannot be taken seriously, nor need they be left in the hands of scholars whose approach to them has largely been rationalistic and spiritually unedifying. Instead, mythology can be understood as first-rate literature that contains a valuable source of knowledge about life and the human psyche, literature with profound psychological and spiritual meaning.

It is not surprising then that a number of Jungian writers have written extensively on the Greek gods and goddesses. For the most part, these writers have used these gods and goddesses as portraits of certain types of personalities. Thus, a "Demeter woman" is a woman whose principal personality configuration is shaped by the archetype of the Great Mother, while an "Aphrodite man or woman" would be a person for whom love and relationship are most essential.[4]

However, a number of goddesses in Greek mythology have been almost entirely overlooked. I call these deities "the lesser-known goddesses of the Greeks." They include the Fates, or Moirae; the Furies, or Erinyes; the various deities who accompanied Aphrodite as part of her retinue, such as the three Graces or Charitēs; the troublesome deity Atē; the awesome deity of necessity, Ananke; and the goddess of all that is uncanny, Hecate. To this list must also be added a deity who bears a masculine name, but who also can be considered as part of the fem-

inine powers because he himself is largely feminine: the god
Dionysus.

There are various reasons why these deities have been
overlooked. One reason is that, except for Dionysus, they represent the older deities of Greek culture; they are goddesses from
the ancient matriarchal era who preceded and were eclipsed by
the more famous Olympian deities such as Apollo, Aphrodite,
Hera, Artemis, Poseidon, Hades, and of course Zeus himself.
These later deities, known as the Olympians, are the deities of
the largely patriarchal era in Greece which succeeded an earlier
matriarchal era. The Olympian deities take all the headlines, as
it were, while the lesser-known goddesses have been relegated
to the background. The Olympian deities also lend themselves
readily to a psychological typology, whereas the more ancient
matriarchal deities do not. It is also easier to learn about the
Olympian deities, for each of them has stories in which they are
the main figures. To find out about the lesser-known goddesses
of the Greeks one must sift through many Greek stories, plays,
and poems—like a goldminer who sifts through the sand that
lies in the bottom of streams—to find and fit together pieces of
information that will once again bring these goddesses to life in
our minds.

There is still another reason why these lesser-known goddesses have been neglected: because the "powers of life" that
they personify have also been neglected. These deities personify
archetypal realities which obtain not so much in individual
human beings and their psychic structure as they obtain in life
itself. Archetypes, we must understand, are living patterns of
life and energy which exist not only in the psychology of people,
but in all nature and in spiritual reality. When we regard these
lesser-known deities, therefore, we are also looking at how life,
nature, and spirit work. This gives these deities a place of primary importance, for it is spiritual life and nature to which all of
us must relate. In fact, while the Olympian deities tend to get the
headlines, it will be one of the major theses of this book that as
far as human life is concerned, these lesser-known deities really
run the show. Furthermore, they ran the show not only as far as
ancient Greece was concerned, but today as well; for these
deities, and the autonomous powers in life and nature which
they depict, determine how life goes on this planet of ours. It is

not too much to say that our very survival as a human community and as a species depends on how we relate to the energies which these ancient deities personify.

We are now ready to meet these goddesses, these deities of old whom we must approach with a receptive and reverent mind, for they are awesome indeed. Perhaps most awesome are the deities of Fate and Necessity, but we will begin our exploration cautiously by looking first at the more gentle of these deities: those lesser-known goddesses who are part of the retinue of the goddess Aphrodite.

Notes

1. The lexicon in which I found a double meaning assigned to this curious word is *The Classic Greek Dictionary* (1901). This old dictionary is unique in that it has both Greek to English and English to Greek sections. A parallel to *kalchainō* is the word *porphureō*. Derived from *porphuresos*, another word for purple or crimson, *porphureō* also has the secondary meaning, "to ponder the deep things of one's mind." A third word with a similar double meaning is *bussodomeuō*, which means literally "to build in the deep," but is also used metaphorically for "to brood over a thing in the depths of one's soul." (For an example of the usage of this word in Greek mythology, see Homer's *Odyssey* 10.309.)
2. This expression is taken from Robert B. Palmer's introduction to Walter Otto's otherwise excellent book *Dionysus: Myth and Cult* (1981), xix.
3. Aeschylus *Agamemnon* 1084: *"menei to theion doulia per en phreni."*
4. As far as I know, the first Jungian analyst to do this work was Philip Zabriskie from New York, whose article "Goddesses in Our Midst" (1974) enriched many of us and inspired others to undertake work of their own.

1

THE RETINUE
OF APHRODITE

$\mathcal{A}$phrodite, goddess of love and erotic desire, is justly famous among the Greek goddesses, but what kind of love is it over which Aphrodite presides? The very question may puzzle us. Is not love, well, just love? What more is there to be said about it? Don't we all know what love is, in a kind of instinctive way that does not require explanation? The Greeks, however, had three words for love; each denoted a special kind of love which was distinct from the other kinds. The word *storgē*, for instance, referred to family love in particular, and devotion and affection generally. The word *agapē*, which the New Testament crowned as the highest kind of love, denotes a love freely given, without thought of recompense; in the Bible, God's love was said to be *agapē*, and the love God wanted from his human creatures was also *agapē*. The third word for love, with which we are most familiar, was *eros*. This word was used for what we would call erotic love, and this love is the special province of Aphrodite. The word *eros* is also the name for Aphrodite's son, the god Eros, of whom we will soon have something to say. So central is *eros* to Aphrodite that in this chapter, unless otherwise specified, when we refer to "love," it will be *eros* we have in mind.

Aphrodite ruled the hearts of both mortals and the gods, all of whom—save the goddesses Athena, Artemis, and Hestia—

were subject to her power to arouse them to love. Under the influence of Aphrodite, desirous love and passion could conquer and inflame the heart even of mighty Zeus, as well as the hearts of the humblest mortal men and women. Less well known is the influence of Aphrodite over all natural life. It was said, for instance, that while the goddess Demeter caused all things to grow, it was Aphrodite who caused the flowers to bloom and the fruit to ripen. For this reason, gardens and flowers were sacred to the goddess—especially the rose, which, with its deep colors and voluptuous, inviting blossoms, was regarded as a holy and unique expression of the essence of the goddess of love herself. The Roman poet Lucretius caught the magic of Aphrodite's power over human beings and animals alike in the moving introduction to his poem "On the Nature of Things." He writes:

> When once the face of the spring day is revealed and the teeming breeze of the west wind is loosed from prison and blows strong, first the birds in high heaven herald thee goddess, and with thine approach, their hearts thrill with thy might. Then the tame beasts grow wild and bound over the fat pastures, and swim the racing rivers; so surely chained by thy charm each follows thee in hot desire whither thou goest before to lead him on. Yea, through seas and mountains and tearing rivers and the leafy haunts of birds and verdant plains thou dost strike fond love into the hearts of all, and makest them in hot desire to renew the stock of their races, each after his own kind. (Lucretius 1992, 1.10ff)

This much is well known. Less known is that when Aphrodite came riding in from the sea, on a great conch shell—arriving from the place where the severed phallus of the Father God Uranus had fallen into the waters, causing the sea to foam and whirl—she was met by a retinue of goddesses. These goddesses received her joyfully, and henceforth accompanied her and tended to her in her comings and goings upon the earth. The first to greet Aphrodite were the three gold-filleted Hours, who clothed her with fine garments. The poet Hesiod tells us:

> They clothed her with heavenly garments; on her head they put a fine, well-wrought crown of gold, and in her

pierced ears they hung gold ornaments, and adorned her
with golden necklaces over her soft neck and snow-white
breasts, jewels which the gold-filleted Hours wear themselves whenever they go to their father's house to join the
lovely dances of the gods. (Hesiod 1982a, 6.5–13)

According to this account, first to greet Aphrodite were the
three Hours; however, other goddesses, anxious to join her retinue, were not far behind. Among these was the goddess Peitho,
known as the goddess of "gentle persuasion": indeed, her very
name comes from a Greek word meaning "winning eloquence
or persuasion." Peitho is the goddess who, under the guidance
and inspiration of Aphrodite, gives to the lover those persuasive
deeds and winning words which enchant the heart and win the
consent of the beloved. Peitho is the deity who especially comes
to help men who wish to win the heart of a woman, because
women more than men, it seems, are won over by the words
they hear; while men, in contrast, are impassioned by the vision
of beauty which they see. Notice, however, that the persuasiveness of Peitho is powerful but gentle; while Peitho's words are
hard to resist, they always seek to win love by consent and
never by force. Lovemaking which is coerced does not belong to
the realm of Aphrodite, since love, if true to itself, must always
be freely given.

Gentle though the persuasiveness of Peitho might be, her
powers are not to be underestimated; she lends to the enchant-
ment of Aphrodite a power of persuasion that can cause the
lover to become oblivious to obligations and to duty. Her energy
lends to Aphrodite the power to bind the heart and will of the
lover not only to the beloved, but to love itself. This is why in
Lucretius's poem the poet says, "so surely *enchained* by thy
charm each follows thee in hot desire whither thou goest before
to lead him on." Peitho's persuasion is a *binding persuasion*,
which overcomes the will and sometimes leads to actions which
later seem incomprehensible to the person whom the goddess of
love desired to *make* submit to her. Hence, the Greek expression,
"Have the courage to love, a god has willed it" (Euripides
1979b, 476).

Therefore, Aphrodite in her aspect as Peitho is the deity of
binding persuasion and compelling power, and for this reason

9

she is associated with chains and cords that symbolize her power: over the heart of a lover, to bind together lover and beloved, and also to bind together soul and body. For this reason, one of the epithets of Aphrodite was "Aphrodite of the chains."

This aspect of the goddess throws light on the many seemingly aberrant fantasies which fill the mind of a person "inspired by Aphrodite." We tend to suppose in our culture that there is, or at least should be, such a thing as good, clean, straightforward lovemaking. The fact is that more people than we might imagine have sexual-erotic fantasies which are kept carefully guarded because they seem so strange. A century or so ago, the fear might have been that the Puritanism of the day would look askance on our sexual fantasies if they were only known. Now it is more likely that a person with certain sexual fantasies might fear being identified in the DSM III (a manual of psychiatric disorders) as "strange," if not positively deranged.

For this reason the sexual-erotic fantasies of many people are kept carefully hidden, often even from the analyst. Many such fantasies involve cords and chains and the like and, therefore, are clinically classified as "masochistic" and something to be "cured." A study of the entourage that accompanied Aphrodite shows, however, that such "erotica" were a natural part of the goddess; in short, they are integral to the nature of the archetype of love that the lore of Aphrodite embodies and expresses. Analyst Lynn Cowan has pointed out in her masterful book, *Masochism: A Jungian View*, that no matter how strange such fantasies may appear, they are nonetheless expressions of the soul's need to "suffer" love.[1] These fantasies symbolize the requirement that the often proud ego *must* submit to all those powers of love, devotion, and pathos that are of true sons and daughters of Aphrodite. For it does appear to be a fact that love and suffering, like love and joy, are never far apart.

Also among those who greeted Aphrodite as she emerged from the sea were three goddesses from whom flowed graciousness and a freely bestowed goodwill. Where love is allowed to be true to itself, it is freely given and carries with it elements of charm and grace. Unsurprisingly, then, Aphrodite was accompanied by three less well-known deities: the Charitēs or "Gracious Ones." That there were three of them, according to

Greek scholar C. Kerényi, is because the Greek mind associated the feminine with the moon, and the moon has three phases: waxing, full, and waning. According to Kerényi, the triadic nature of the Charitēs or Graces, and the triadic nature of other goddesses as well, is no accident; they form a Trinity, a genuine three-in-one, comparable to the Christian trinity of God as Father, Son, and Holy Spirit: three distinct "persons" but one essence.[2] The name of these three goddesses—the Charitēs—comes from the Greek verb *charein*—to rejoice—and from the noun *charis*, which refers to a grace or favor that is freely given.[3] The word *charis* is the same word used in the New Testament for the "grace of God," seen by the early Christians as a favor which God bestowed on humankind freely, a pouring-forth of the abundance of divine love.

In keeping with their gracious nature, the individual names of the Charitēs were Aglaea, which means "splendid beauty"; Euphrosyne, which means "glad thoughts, good cheer"; and Thalaia, which means "abundance, plenty." It is also interesting that while the Charitēs were generally thought to be the daughters of Zeus by his third wife, Euryphnome, some said that they were the daughters of the river god Lethē, whose name means "a forgetting or oblivion." This suggests that the Charitēs joined with Peitho in leading mortals into a lovemaking in which not only the sorrows and pains of everyday life, but also the usual boundaries established by duty, loyalty, and obligation, might be dissolved in the oblivion and rapture of the love embrace.

We have already mentioned that while Demeter made plants grow, the touch of Aphrodite brought their blossoms. This she accomplished through the Charitēs, whose touch caused the flourishing plant to bud and then to bloom. It was also the touch of the Charitēs which caused the fruit to ripen on the trees. This aspect of the Charitēs is especially interesting, since it says something about the importance of letting a potential love relationship "ripen" before picking the fruit of lovemaking. If we eat the fruit of the tree before it is ready, eating it may leave us with only a sour, bitter taste or an empty feeling; what is more, it may prove indigestible. The goddess of love and the Charitēs who accompany her cannot be coerced or hurried into giving us the pleasure or fruits we desire, for while it is true

11

that gifts of love are freely given, it is also true that their ripening cannot be forced.

The Charitēs also had a kinship with the three Muses, the deities of music, song, dance, poetry, and eloquent speech from whose name we derive such English words as *music, musician,* and *museum,* as well as the verb "to muse." Like the three Muses, the Charitēs loved to dance, and they were especially wont to dance together on a clear, moonlit night. Greek art often represented this triad of three-goddesses-in-one holding hands or lightly touching each other on the shoulder as they danced in a line or circle, scantily but becomingly clad in their *chitons* or gowns. Thus, along with the Muses, the Charitēs bestowed upon the world the gifts of beauty, binding love, and also memory—for what true lover has ever forgotten a love?

Because of their love of the dance, the Charitēs were also close in heart and spirit to the god Dionysus who, as we will see in a later chapter, brought his followers the gifts of divine mania and ecstasy. Suffice it for now to say that under the influence of Dionysus, mortals abandoned their usual scruples and mores, experiencing ecstatic joy when their usual ego structures were creatively dissolved in the magical power of the god. Likewise, Aphrodite offers her devotees at least a glimpse of such ecstasy in the rapture of the love embrace to which the Charitēs invite us.

A special function of the Charitēs was to tend to the toilet of the goddess of love, bathing her and anointing her body with oil and sweet perfumes. When Aphrodite wanted to make love to the mortal man Anchises, we are told "there the Graces bathed her with heavenly oil such as blooms upon the bodies of the eternal gods—oil divinely sweet, which she had by her, filled with fragrance" (Hesiod 1982a, 61–3). Likewise, after Aphrodite's scandalous love affair with Ares, during which her vengeful husband Hephaestus cast his intricately made net over the two lovers when he caught them lying together in their illicit embrace, we are told that the Charitēs "bathed her and anointed her with immortal oil, such as gleams upon the gods that are forever. And they clothed her in lovely raiment, a wonder to behold" (Homer 1984, 8.364–5). Thus, all fashion, seductive ointments, and perfumes, indeed anything which adds charm and grace to the way in which others perceive us or we perceive ourselves, derives its inspiration from the Charitēs.

12

If we consider the Charitēs as the threefold manifestation of a single deity, then the third goddess to be considered as one of the retinue of Aphrodite was the goddess Aidos, the deity of modesty, self-respect, *and* shame. Indeed, so closely were Aphrodite and Aidos associated that it was said that wherever the goddess of love went, Aidos would not be far behind. The close association in the Greek imagination of love and shame that is seen in the companionship of Aphrodite and Aidos may surprise us today; in our culture we have tried our best to eliminate any element of shame from sexuality, as well as to devalue the element of modesty in lovemaking. Have we not learned from psychology that we are not to be ashamed of our sexuality, that to feel shame about sex is to repress it and incur a neurosis as a consequence? Are we not finally free from the dark shadow cast on lovemaking by our puritanical ancestors, so that we may now enjoy the free unrestricted expression of our sexuality without the burden of guilt or shame? Have not many of us cast our eyes longingly back on ancient Greek culture as a time in which sexuality and the body and the instincts were freely expressed, without the joy-killing burden of a puritanical Christianity said to oppose all the joys of the flesh?

In our present culture, we do indeed seem free of such encumbrances on our pleasures as shame, for not only is sex-without-shame to be enjoyed in our private lives, it also now exists in our public life. Today we can go to the movies and watch handsome, perfectly proportioned, naked lovers make perfect love in front of our eyes without a hint of shame to deprive us of our pleasure. If we were honest with ourselves, though, we might feel a bit less than adequate, since our bodies and our lovemaking do not always measure up to the ideal lovemaking the movies are suggesting to us we too should achieve. Similarly, garb once characteristic of streetwalkers—such as high boots and tight-fitting dresses—has now become the fashion of the day. Our joy in sex is unrestrained, except for the nagging feeling of inferiority some of us may have that we, poor mortals that we are, are not the perfect lovers with perfect bodies that the godlike actors and actresses are in our films.

Our culture has gone to great lengths to cast aside modesty and shame, efforts aimed first at lifting sexual repression and now dedicated to achieving the maximum amount of sexual

13

pleasure. It may come as a surprise to learn that Aphrodite, goddess of love and sexual pleasure par excellence, was accompanied by her consort deity Aidos, the goddess of shame. Modern psychology and our contemporary culture notwithstanding, the wisdom of the Greeks said that just as Aphrodite and Aidos travel together, so also where there is true love and joyous lovemaking a certain element of shame and modesty must also be present. This is why Aidos was also said to be the daughter of the goddess Nuks (Night) for Aidos was said to guard with her dark wings the secrets of love and lovers, because love belonged to the *yin*-like darkness, not to the glaring *yang* of bright sunlight.

When it comes to the realm of animal life, the way of Aphrodite and Aidos seems to prevail in a natural way. For the most part, the sexual life of birds and other animals is closely regulated by nature. In the spring, for instance, when Aphrodite blesses life and spreads her magic through the world of nature, the bull elk mates with as many of the cows as possible, thus guaranteeing the survival of the species. When spring is over, sexual expression retires into the background until spring returns and once more the goddess touches the land. As a rule the sexual life of animals is so closely guarded—to use our mythological language, so sheltered by Aidos—that it is difficult to observe. For instance, bird watchers who have tried to study the sexual life of magpies report considerable frustration. It seems that these crow-like birds, usually raucous and conspicuous in their behavior, are almost impossible to observe during the mating season. This is because male and female birds make love so hidden in the foliage of large-leaved trees that even the most voyeuristic of bird watchers has difficulty seeing what they are up to. Snakes also fall into this category. It is a rare occasion when snakes can be observed mating because many of them pair off in hidden places such as caves.

The sexual life of wolves and coyotes is especially interesting. Naturalists tell us that under ordinary conditions, only the alpha male and alpha female in the pack will mate. This modest approach to lovemaking prevails until an unusual number of wolves or coyotes begin to die off—from disease, perhaps, or more likely from the bullets, poison, and relentless harassment of human beings. When this happens, the signal goes out that *all* the males and females are to mate. In this way the chances for the survival of the pack are greatly increased. This may be one reason why coyotes, although hated, hunted, poisoned, and destroyed by human beings in every imaginable way, have actually increased in number to the point where they now exist in parks and open spaces in our cities, and have migrated to places—like New England—where they were not known to have existed before.[4] All of which is a way of saying that Aphrodite and Aidos not only give joyous expression to love and sexuality; they also regulate it. Of course, there are exceptions to the closely regulated sexual life we see in the animal kingdom. Baboons, for instance, can be observed having quick and indiscriminate sexual intercourse almost any time of day or night.

Plato took all of this into account in his discussion of love. Aphrodite, he notes in the *Symposium*, is twofold: there is the heavenly Aphrodite and the vulgar or common Aphrodite.[5] Eros, the god of love who is himself the son of Aphrodite and who is often her close consort, may urge us to make love that is either noble or base. Plato writes of this:

> For when the doing of it [love] is noble and right, the thing itself becomes noble; when wrong, it becomes base. So also it is with loving, and Love [Eros] is not in every case noble or worthy of celebration, but only when he impels us to love in a noble manner. (1984e, 181A)

Of course, everyone has their own ideas of what constitutes noble love and what constitutes base love. From the Greek point of view, the distinguishing feature is whether or not the goddess Aidos and all that she represents is present in the lovemaking. The sense of modesty and capacity for shame that Aidos brings enhances rather than diminishes love and lovemaking. The absence of Aidos, as we have noted, is not freedom from shame but shamelessness. The presence of Aidos actually brings with it a certain sensitivity which heightens the joy of love, for where Aidos is present, there Aphrodite also dwells, bringing with her the pleasures of body *and* soul. One connection between Aidos and the body is seen in the Greek word for genitals. The male genitals were termed *aidolo*, which is the dual word for *aidos*;

15

literally, the Greek word for the genitals of a man or woman means "things over which modesty is felt" (Cf. Plato 1984e, 190A3).

An important way in which *aidos* enhances the secrets of love and lovemaking, which intensifies enjoyment, is reflected in the intimacy of lovers. Lovers whose relationship is personal—a "secret" hidden from others, an intimate sharing—participate in the goddess Aidos. When secret ways of making love are shared between lovers, the goddess is certainly present, and these secret ways promote that quality of intimacy which makes the experience of love special and important.

There is another form of shame, however, which is deadly, not only to the soul but sometimes to our very existence. There is hardly a more painful experience in life than to be ashamed of oneself. In certain cultures, a person who felt this kind of shame might take his or her own life rather than live in disgrace in the eyes of his or her compatriots. This shame brings with it a "loss of face" with oneself and in the presence of others. A shame like this, however, is not expressed in Greek by the word *aidos* but by the word *aischros*, which denotes something ugly, deformed, and utterly disgraceful. That which is *aischros*, says Plato, has nothing to do with the true mysteries of Eros.[6]

Ancient Greeks lived in what anthropologists call a shame culture rather than a guilt culture. The shame of *aischros* was devastating, as Greek scholar E. R. Dodds has pointed out, for the goal in ancient Greece was not to bask in the enjoyment of a quiet conscience but in the enjoyment of public esteem (1957, 17). It is this kind of devastating shame which psychotherapists may have to help their patients contend with, if they were afflicted with it as the result of abusively moralistic parents, and/or an overdose of moralizing religious influences that imbued in the child not a healthy respect for *aidos*, but a crushing feeling of *aischros*.

Among many Native American people, this kind of shame was the most terrible experience for a person. Even today, if we act in a truly shameful way, we may suffer deeply. What in Jungian psychology we call the "persona" is at work here. Our persona is the way we want other people to see us; it is the "face" we put on that enables us to meet our fellow human beings. If we "lose face" with those people whose esteem we value, then our psychological functioning may be seriously impaired. If such a thing happened to an ancient Greek, then, as we noted, suicide might be the result; even today, suicides caused by a devastating "loss of face" do take place. Worse than this social disgrace, however, is the sense of dishonor that comes to a person who is ashamed of himself or herself because of an action they consider disgraceful. This dishonor, however, can come only to a person who has certain principles in the first place. If a person lives life without spiritual or moral convictions, that is, without any principles, then that person is "shameless," "without Aidos." If a person does have principles, and then betrays them through recklessness, selfishness, or cowardice, then deep suffering can result.

Now we can understand why the goddess Aidos was for the Greeks the goddess of self-respect, as well as the goddess of shame. The psychology is that if we lack the capacity for shame, we also lack the capacity for self-respect. That Aidos closely accompanies Aphrodite tells us that the capacities for shame and self-respect, for modesty and love, go together. In this way, Aidos is that power which restrains people from doing what is wrong, or what is against the moral ideals of the group. If people transgress against Aidos, then they are either ashamed of themselves or experience shame in front of their peers, or both. On the other hand, as we have seen, to be without Aidos is to be "shameless"; and without the moderating influences of shame and self-respect, human beings are capable of the most incredible evil. When that happens, so Hesiod tells us,

> Aidos and Nemesis, with their sweet forms wrapped in white robes, will go from the wide-pathed earth and forsake humankind to join the company of the deathless gods: and bitter sorrows will be left for mortals, and there will be no help against evil.[7]

A concrete example of the power and reality of Aidos can be found in the act of blushing. Imagine a boy who is on the threshold of becoming a man. All kinds of glandular changes are taking place in him, and with them come many new and strange emotions. One change is that he finds himself now noticing, indeed, being fascinated by, the young lady across the

17

street. Before she had only been a playmate, or perhaps the object of his boyish scorn or teasing; but now he finds himself strangely drawn to her. In fact, he cannot seem to keep from thinking about her. The truth is that he is in love for the first time in his life. He feels so shy and strange about this (*aidos*) that he keeps his affections and fantasies about the girl a closely guarded secret; but, alas! his "secret" is no secret, for his affections for the young lady betray themselves to others every time he sees her. Then let us imagine that one day—when the young man is gazing furtively on the girl across the street, enraptured by the fantasies that Aphrodite is putting into his mind—a "wicked" older brother or sister, who sees perfectly clearly what is happening, teases him in front of others about his affections. Our young man's reaction? A deep, involuntary, and conspicuous reddening spreads over his face—he has blushed, and in his blush, to his agony, his love is revealed for all to see.

Blushing is a demonstration that the archetypes live in the body as well as in the soul. Putting the matter more scientifically: the archetypes are *so real* that they manifest themselves in the central nervous system as well as in the images and fantasies that go through our minds. We also need to note, however, that blushing mostly occurs in a young person whose soul is still pure. When the soul has become jaded—and this seems to happen all too early nowadays—such a spontaneous manifestation of Aidos is no longer possible. The goddess, with her saving if sometimes painful sense of modesty, has departed.

By preserving the sanctity of the soul, Aidos also helps the soul remain a fitting home for the divine. This enables the love and lovemaking inspired in us by Aphrodite to be a religious and spiritual experience as well as a sensual and sexual one. Combined, Aidos and Aphrodite keep sexual love numinous, numinosity being that profound feeling we have in the presence of that which is awe-inspiring, holy, and thus divine. Shielded and protected from profane eyes by Aidos, Aphrodite and her divine realm are with lovers the world over. If Aphrodite is separated from her companion Aidos, though, the subtle and divine nature of the eros which the goddess of love can inspire in us will be absent. Thus Aidos, as Lynn Cowan has pointed out, holds together the sexual and the religious, the ecstatic and the divine, for "Aidos maintains that secrecy and privacy of sex which mark it as sacramental" (Cowan 1982, 112).

As we have seen, when Aphrodite and her companion goddesses touch the hearts of living creatures, animals and human beings alike, then "love we must for a god has willed it." Note the word *must*, for hidden in love lies the *necessity* to love. This element of necessity leads us to the next goddess we consider: "great Ananke," goddess of Necessity herself.

Notes

1. Cowan 1982, 26. Cowan writes, "When masochism is literal only, it is pathological. Without its sense of worship and submission, without acknowledgment of the god moving in it, masochism loses its connection to, and meaning for, the soul."
2. Kerényi 1951, 31. Cf. also 36, 38, 40.
3. From the Greek word *charis*, meaning a grace, loveliness, kindness, or boon. Our word *charity* comes from this Greek word; but in our culture, charity tends to imply something given with condescension. The Greek word implies something given without thought of recompense and without any depreciation of the recipient. It is used in this way in the New Testament to describe the love of God toward humankind.
4. Another reason for the survival rate of coyotes is because they are omnivorous. Wolves, on the other hand, restrict their diet to meat.
5. Plato 1984e, 180D, 181A–B. "Public, common, vulgar."
6. Ibid. 197B. Plato says that Apollo invented archery and medicine under the guidance of love (Eros), and that Love also guided the Muses to make music and Hephaestus in his craftsmanship, but "Love has no concern with ugliness" (*aisxei gar ouk epi Eros*).
7. Hesiod 1982b, 197–201. Nemesis is the goddess of "righteous indignation."

2

$\mathcal{A}$NANKE AND
THE $\mathcal{D}$AIMŌNES

$\mathcal{W}$e have already noted the statement in Euripides' play *Hippolytus*, "Have the courage to love, a god has willed it." To the Greek mind, what a god has willed we *must* do, or pay a grievous penalty. Psychologically, this compelling power of the gods is a mythological way of describing the power of the archetypes over the human ego. In this "will of the gods" lies the element of *necessity*, a factor in our lives which we human beings often want to avoid, but which holds us in an implacable grip.

Considering the power of necessity over us, it is not surprising to discover that the Greeks had a goddess of necessity: "Great Ananke: Necessity herself" (Harrison 1955, 592). The necessity denoted by the word *ananke* includes all necessities imposed upon us from either outer demands and constraints, or necessities imposed from within ourselves by the inexorable demands of our own needs and nature. For the Greeks this also included the constraining ties of blood, relationship, and kindred.

Like other Greek deities, Ananke has an affinity to many of the other goddesses. She is especially closely related to the goddess Themis and to the three Moirae, or Fates, all of whom we will consider in a later chapter. Although never a permanent part of the retinue of Aphrodite, Ananke nevertheless also had a certain affinity to the goddess of love. For Aphrodite, as we have seen, imposed the necessity to love on men and women, birds and beasts, on everything that flies, swims, creeps, crawls, and even on the gods themselves. For this reason, as discussed above, she was associated with chains and ties of all sorts, because we are "bound" to love.

Ananke embraces the most humble of necessities and the most sublime, the necessities of the body and those of the spirit. According to Plato, Ananke was the power at work in those early dealings of the gods related by Hesiod before even the power of Love emerged; her power was imposed on gods and mortals from the very beginning.[1] Even the wayward god of war Ares had to heed the power of Ananke, who was called "Necessity, whom not the god of war withstands" (Plato 1984e, 196D). Another necessity Ananke lays upon us is the necessity to create in whatever way is appropriate for us, for when creative energy is not expressed, then it turns against us. To understand how our creativity works from a psychological viewpoint, it helps to understand the important role played in our lives by what the Greeks called the *daimōn*.

The idea of the *daimōn* goes very far back in Greek history; we find an early description of the *daimōnes* in Hesiod, who refers to them as "pure spirits dwelling on the earth." He says they are kindly and are "guardians of mortals." They roam everywhere throughout the earth, though they are hard to see since they are "clothed in mist," keeping an eye out for those who commit cruel deeds, and bestowing wealth on those whom they favor (Hesiod 1982b, 122–6). Initially in Greek mythology, a *daimōn* was experienced as a driving force or energy which readily lent itself to personification. As Jane Harrison has pointed out, Eros is such a power, more like a *daimōn* than a god, a driving energy inspiring and compelling animals and human beings alike to love and participate in the creation of new life. Thus, Aphrodite, Eros her son, and Ananke are all connected.

As a spiritual power greater than a human being but less than a god, one of the principal functions of the *daimōn* is to mediate between the divine realm of the gods and the human realm of mortals. Socrates, in speaking of Eros as a *daimōn*, emphasized this ability of the *daimōn* to move between the divine realm and the human realm, and its function to relate the two. Speaking of Eros, which he called a *daimōn megas*—powerful spirit—he said that Love (Eros) is always:

Interpreting and transporting human beings to the gods and divine things to men; entreaties and sacrifices from below, and ordinances and requitals from above; being midway between it makes each to supplement the other, so that the whole is combined in one . . . For God [*Theos*] with men does not mingle, but the spiritual [*daimōnion*] is the means of all society and converse of men with gods and of gods with men, whether waking or sleeping. (Plato 1984e, 203A)

From its early origin as an extra-human power, the idea of the *daimōn* appears to have evolved to that of a spiritual power which could have an individual relationship to a human being. Plato especially regarded the *daimōn* as a quasi-divine power which could have an individual relationship to the human soul. When, for instance, a person died, it was the *daimōn* of that person, who had been assigned to him from the beginning as a guide, which took the soul to its proper place in the underworld. Plato writes:

And so it was said that after death the tutelary genius [*daimōn*] of each person, to whom he had been allotted in life, leads him to a place where the dead are gathered together; then they are judged and depart to the other world with the guide [*daimōn*] whose task it is to conduct thither those who come from this world. (1984c, 107D)

As the tutelary spirit of a person, the *daimōn* could have an important relationship to the soul in life as well as being the soul's guide in the underworld. Socrates, for instance, tells us about his personal *daimōn*, and how it was the source of his philosophical inspiration. Regarding his capacity to come up with inspired ideas, Socrates says:

But the reason for this . . . is that something divine and spiritual (*daimōnion*) comes to me . . . I have had this from my childhood; it is a sort of voice that comes to me, and when it comes it always holds me back from what I am thinking of doing but never urges me forward. This it is which opposes my engaging in politics. (Plato 1984a, 31D)

The unique relationship which Socrates had with his *daimōn* created in him such a creative and free-thinking personality that he

23

got into difficulty with the authorities, who accused him of introducing new divinities into the minds of people and thus creating disbelief in the established traditions of the state. On the basis of this accusation, Socrates was condemned to die, for he refused to recant his faith in his *daimōn* and preferred death to a slavery of the mind. It was not only Socrates' beliefs that brought him trouble with the authorities, but also the uniqueness of his personality, which disquieted those of a more collective spirit; Socrates' relationship with his *daimōn* made him not only an original thinker, but also what we would call today an individuated person. Such people have often been perceived as a threat by people still encased in collective attitudes.

The Romans took over the Greek idea of the *daimōn*, as they did so many Greek ideas, and translated the word *daimōn* by the Latin word *genius*. This word has come down into English to denote an exceptionally brilliant person, like Einstein, but it was originally used in a more general way, the notion being that everyone had a power and inspiration in him/her and that the source of this power was the person's "genius." Indeed, the *genius* was so closely related to the personality that sometimes the distinction is blurred. For this reason, the Graeco-Latin mind pictured a rivalry or enmity between two people as a rivalry or contest between their respective geniuses. An interesting example is given by the Roman biographer Plutarch, who described the rivalry between the Roman Emperor Octavius (later known as Caesar Augustus) and the Roman general Mark Antony as a contest between their geniuses, a contest, Plutarch pointed out, which Antony's genius was bound to lose. Plutarch writes:

> But it annoyed Antony that in all their arguments or any trial of skill or fortune, Caesar should be constantly victorious . . . He (Antony) had with him an Egyptian diviner, one of those who calculate nativities, who . . . declared to him that though the fortune that attended to him was bright and glorious, yet it was over-shadowed by Caesar's; and advised him to keep himself as far distant as he could from that young man; "for your genius," said he, "dreads his; when absent from him your genius is proud and brave, but in his presence unmanly and dejected," and incidents that occurred to him appeared to show that the Egyptian spoke the truth. For whenever they cast lots

for any playful purpose, or threw dice, Antony was still
the loser; and repeatedly, when they fought game-cocks or
quails, Caesar's [genius] had the victory.[2]

History proved the Egyptian correct; in the Battle of Actium the
forces of Antony were badly beaten by those of Octavius, and
this defeat led eventually to Antony's suicide.

The idea of the *daimōn* or "genius" was a fundamental part
of ancient psychology, for one could not understand what a person was all about until you knew the nature of his or her genius.
Today, however, this way of understanding a person has all but
vanished. Part of the reason for this may be that the Christians
confused the idea of the *daimōn* with something necessarily evil.
Now, it is true that some people had a *daimōn* who could lead
them into evil. E. R. Dodds points out that a *daimōn* might even
produce that state of moral confusion and irrational behavior
that the Greeks called *atē* (a state we will consider more deeply
in another chapter). Some people do in fact seem to have in them
a "genius" for doing evil, for which reason—no matter how
much they are punished for their crimes and no matter how
much rehabilitation is tried—they persist in crime all their lives.

Since the *daimōn* is a function of the unconscious, this may
be one reason that many people are suspicious of the whole idea
of the unconscious, as though ignoring the reality of the unconscious might make it go away. The early Christian philosopher
Tertullian, for example, in a discussion of demons, says of
Socrates that from an early age he was "found by the spirit of
the demon." He continues, "Thus, too, is it that to all persons
their *genii* are assigned, which is only another name for demons.
Hence in no case—I mean of the heathens of course—is there
any nativity which is pure of idolatrous superstition"(Tertullian
1957, 3.39).

More strange than the fact that early Christianity was suspicious of the idea of the *daimōn* is that contemporary psychology has by-and-large no place in it for the idea of the *daimōn* or
genius within us. Jung and some of his colleagues have noted the
idea, but give it only passing mention; the only important reference from Jung comes from one of his seminars on dream analysis in which he discusses briefly the Greeks' idea that everyone
had a *daimōn* and that this idea was carried over by the Romans

25

into their idea of the genius. Jung cites the example of Socrates, which we have already noted, and observed that the *daimōn/genius* was powerful, but in itself was neither good nor bad. He went on to note that in those ancient times it was commonly supposed that everyone had a *sunopados* (companion) who accompanied them, and that this is the origin of a person's abiding genius. Marie-Louise von Franz extended this idea a bit further, suggesting that the basic idea of the *daimōn/genius* was a way of representing a person's relationship to the Self.

Despite the early Christian prejudice against the idea of the *daimōn/genius*, the essential thought of it found its way into Christianity in the idea of the guardian angel, appointed by God at the moment of the soul's conception to be that soul's help and aid and guide through life. This idea is very much like Plato's idea of the *daimōn* as a helpful companion to the ego. This belief in the guardian angel appeared quite early in Christian thought and became widespread. Somewhat later in Christianity, various of the saints acquired the status of independent spiritual powers who, like the *daimōnes*, were more than human, though less than God. The saints offer help, guidance, and inspiration to the soul through a person's life, and in times of distress or confusion a person can pray to his or her special saint for help. Many of these functions of the angels and the saints in Christian thought are analogous to the old idea of the *daimōn* or genius.

Another idea comparable to that of the *daimōn/genius* is the belief in the Ancestors, a belief very much alive today in most of Africa. South of the Sahara Desert the belief is that if a person lived a long and exemplary life, then at death that person might be appointed by Umlukulu (the Zulu name for God) to be one of the Ancestors. It was the function of the Ancestors to offer guidance and correction to human beings. They especially tried to keep a person on the right path in life, and to help that person avoid sickness and evil. If a person began to go the wrong way in life, then the Ancestors might send warnings through dreams in which they might appear in theriomorphic form, often as serpents; if the warnings were not heeded then the dreams might intensify; ordinary dreams could become nightmares, and in still more serious cases the cattle might begin to die, a person might have an accident, or some still more serious misfortune might occur.[3] In such ways did the ancients and people from other cultures than our own anticipate the belief in the power of the unconscious not only to be the source of creativity and assistance, but also to correct us when we stray from the right path in life—by sending warning dreams at night, and through adverse incidents which might occur in our waking hours.

The idea of the *daimōn/genius* is especially important for a complete psychological typology. Jungian psychology has done a great deal for typology with its theory of extraversion and introversion, and the four functions of thinking and feeling, sensation and intuition; but this is not enough. We also need to know the nature of our genius if we are to understand what we are all about. If, for instance, you have a genius for building houses or putting automobile engines together, you must pursue a very different course in life than if you have a genius for art or psychotherapy. Many young people especially flounder badly in their early adult lives because they have not yet identified their genius, or because the ambitions of their genius have been thwarted by inner or outer life circumstances.

There is also a relationship between the *daimōn/genius* and our sleep and dreams. If, for instance, we are confronted in our waking hours with a problem which we cannot resolve, our *daimōn/genius* will work on the problem while we are asleep. That is why the adage "sleep on it" is psychologically sound; in our sleep the *daimōn/genius* within us often works out a solution to a problem we cannot solve, so that when we awaken in the morning, a problem that seemed unresolvable the night before now has a clear answer.

It is also during our sleep, sometimes directly through our dreams, that the *daimōn/genius* may give us a new and inventive idea that would never have occurred to us in waking life. Robert Louis Stevenson, for instance, tells us that the plot for his famous novelette *Dr. Jekyll and Mr. Hyde* came to him in a dream. In this dream there were two distinctly different figures, one seemingly good and one clearly evil. Stevenson tells us that his story *Dr. Jekyll and Mr. Hyde* came from this dream, and the central motif of the story, the transformation of the "good" Dr. Jekyll to the sinister Mr. Hyde, was taken directly from it.

For the genius to operate successfully, however, requires the cooperation of the ego. Education and training, for instance, will likely be essential for the creative functioning of the genius.

Someone might have a genius for performing surgery, but without extensive medical training and experience, the potential of the genius cannot be fulfilled. This is one reason why education is such an important part of psychological development. It also illustrates the way a creative working relationship develops between the conscious development of the ego and the unconscious creative functioning of the *daimōn/genius*.

Sometimes the figure of the genius appears directly in a dream. One man, for instance, reported a dream in which he came across some gold coins. At the moment in the dream when the dreamer discovered the gold coins, another man, unknown to the dreamer, appeared from below the ground, took the coins, and disappeared with them. The dreamer understood this unknown figure to be that of the genius, and the coins to be the archetypal values and insights which he had recently acquired. Just as the Greek god of creative work and craft, Hephaestus, had a forge under the earth where his inventiveness flourished, so this man in the dream seemed to have a hidden place in the underground of the unconscious where he engaged in the work of the creative imagination. Robert Louis Stevenson, for instance, relates in his autobiography that he did not write his stories. Rather, they were the creations of his "little people"; they did the creative work and came up with the plots and the ideas, and he simply wrote things down and refined them a little.

This idea of the "little people" as symbols of the creative genius at work in the night is well expressed in the fairy tale "The Elves and the Shoemaker." In this tale a hardworking but poor shoemaker is reduced to such poverty that he has only enough leather left for one more pair of shoes, and then it is all over with him. Saddened by his impoverished state of affairs, he goes to sleep knowing that in the morning he will be making his last pair of shoes. When he awakens, however, he finds that the leather he left on the table has been fashioned into an amazingly beautiful and skillfully crafted pair of shoes. So well made and appealing are these shoes that the shoemaker has no difficulty in selling them for a considerable sum of money, with which he feeds his family, leaving plenty of money with which to buy more leather. Once again when the shoemaker goes to sleep, he leaves the leather on the worktable, and once again when he awakens in the morning, he finds an artfully crafted pair of shoes has been made out of the leather he left. Indeed, this time there are several pairs of shoes because the leather was so plentiful.

These shoes he also sells for a great deal of money, and this time when he goes to sleep, he can leave more leather on the worktable, all of which he finds in the morning has been made into wonderful shoes. This goes on for some time until the shoemaker becomes well-to-do. Eventually, however, the shoemaker becomes curious about the mysterious powers which work so diligently and creatively at night on his behalf, so he stays awake to watch what happens. What should appear in the dead of the night but the elves, who quickly and deftly set to work to make wonderful shoes from the leather. But, alas! when the elves realize they are being watched, they vanish—never to appear again!

The elves personify the creative genius of the shoemaker; they work at night, for they are a predominantly unconscious functioning. The negative effect that occurs when the elves realize they are being watched can be understood as a symbol of what happens when our creative process is made too rational, or when the ego gets in the way by trying to control the creative process in order to fulfill its own egocentric ambitions.

The story of "The Elves and the Shoemaker" shows that one of the many necessities imposed upon us, at least for many people, is the necessity to create; for unless we create we are impoverished psychologically and spiritually, not to mention economically. Thus, the "have to's" of life, which are expressive of the reality of Ananke, include the necessity to create. In creating, our "genius" is expressed and fulfilled; without creating, the "genius" is frustrated and may well turn against us and cause psychological problems, as though Ananke herself was angry at us for failing to bring to fruition what lies in our nature to do.

More often than not we object to Ananke and the demands she puts upon us, for the ego, as long as it is caught in its egocentricity, wants to do what *it* wants to do. Consequently, as we have observed, necessity is often the object of our complaints, and sometimes considerable time and energy is spent by people trying to free themselves from Ananke's iron grip. At election time in the United States we hear often of something called the "American dream." Just what this American dream is does not get spelled out, but often it appears to be nothing more than becoming so financially successful that we can be free of the necessity to work, and so can devote ourselves completely to leisure. Yet, should we be so unfortunate as to become free from financial and other necessities in life, we are likely to find that our lives go awry in mysterious ways. It is as though Ananke, offended because she has been banished, reappears, hidden in a host of bedeviling psychological or physical symptoms or unnerving outer circumstances to which we *must* pay attention.

If we should become free from the necessity to work, we are called upon to face another necessity: the need to find a creative life appropriate to our particular personality. Otherwise we may develop negative symptoms: drinking too much, a boredom which can only be alleviated by increasingly addictive excitements, relationships which eventually deteriorate because we are demanding too much of them, and eventually, perhaps, threats to our health. Here we have a paradox: at the very point when the ego supposes that it is now "free," it is in the most danger. The only real freedom is to serve the Divine Being, of whom Ananke is a living part.

Ananke is also an important clinical element in certain psychological disorders. She is to be found, for instance, in addictive disorders such as alcoholism and drug addiction. In such cases the victim of the disorder experiences a powerful compulsion amounting to a necessity to drink or ingest a drug. The experience of the addictive personality is that he or she *must* get more and more of the addictive substance in order to experience a cessation of pain or feeling of well-being. The essence of the cure for most people with such addictive disorders is substituting a positive necessity for the negative necessity of the addictive substance. The positive necessity might be or include regular attendance at meetings of Alcoholics Anonymous or analogous organizations, plus a devotion to the sound spiritual and psychological principles of such groups. The difference between a negative necessity (addiction) and a positive necessity (helping programs) is that while the former is destructive, the latter lead to personal growth, greater consciousness, and the development of character, as suffering individuals learn to devote themselves to living by certain life principles.

Another psychological disorder in which Ananke is conspicuously involved is known in psychiatry as obsessive compulsive disorder (OCD). Victims of this distressing disorder are compelled to engage in apparently fruitless ritualistic and repetitive behavior patterns, which *must* be performed in just such a way and which serve no useful purpose except to temporarily relieve the patient from the suffering and impediment to action which continue until the appropriate ritual is performed. The individual suffering from such a compulsion dislikes the rituals intensely, and performs them against his or her will only because there is no other way to find relief.

Instances of OCD may be so mild that they may scarcely merit classification as a psychiatric disturbance. For instance, after people speak openly about some good fortune that has come to them, they may, partly in jest but also partly seriously, "knock on wood." This "superstition" goes back to the times in which people actively believed in the devil. The idea was that the devil might hear what was said about someone's good fortune and come to take it away by wrecking havoc in that person's life. The wood on which a person knocked was originally regarded as the wood of the Cross of Christ, which alone had the power to avert the machinations of the Evil One, who was so jealous of human well-being and happiness.

Such a hangover from humankind's more superstitious days hardly merits a psychiatric classification, but in other cases matters become more serious. Someone might, for instance, suffer from a compulsion to check the stove repeatedly to make sure the fire is out before being able to go to sleep. Checking the stove once to make sure it is turned off is a good precaution, but if it is repeated ten or twenty or a hundred times, then Ananke has made her appearance in a negative way.

For this reason, obsessive compulsive disorder can be a serious psychiatric condition because it limits life so much and imposes such a torturous necessity on its victims. In the case of one person who came to me for help for this disorder (and with whose permission I relate this case), the rituals to be performed took up many hours of the day, interfering drastically with her work, her family life, and her self-esteem. She experienced these rituals as an absolute requirement forced upon her by dark

powers which promised to exact vengeance upon her by insti-
gating accidents, for instance, unless the rituals were performed.

In the case of this young woman, significant relief of symptoms was achieved by substituting active imagination for the rituals. The active imaginations also *had to be done* if she was to be
free of the life-defeating compulsion, but they took much less
time than the rituals she was originally compelled to perform,
and also led her in a most interesting way into a meaningful
experience with her inner world. We could say that the cure for
this woman still required service to be rendered to Ananke,
because the active imagination was obligatory if she was to
experience any relief from her compulsions, but since she had
found a creative way to render such service, she experienced a
positive benefit.

The active imagination performed by this woman is a form
of what could be called "inner work." Many people who are
technically "symptom free" find that their lives go much better
when inner psychological and spiritual work is regularly performed. It would seem that, just as the body has certain needs
which *must* be satisfied, so also does the soul have such needs if
it is to remain healthy and creative.

The necessity for mortals to serve the gods is why the
Greeks also associated Ananke with healing, for when a person
realizes that she or he *must* live in a certain way, then Ananke is
served and health can come. When, for instance, we realize that
we must put the right kind of food into our bodies to remain
healthy, then health of body (and soul) can come. When we
know that we must either live creatively or fall into depression,
then spiritual health can come. When the alcoholic realizes that
she or he must live a psychologically honest life or be compelled
to drink, then the cure is possible. So is it that health of body and
soul is achieved through adhering to the demands of Ananke,
the living archetype of "what must be done."

Further, the idea that the cure for many of our afflictions
lies in the creative acceptance of necessity is an integral part of
that process of becoming a whole person that C. G. Jung called
"individuation." While Dr. Jung identified the individuation
process and described it, he did not, of course, invent it. There
are, in fact, "case histories" of persons who went through individuation going back in time at least as far as the biblical stories

of Jacob and Joseph, and perhaps the first person to teach about this process in all of its psychological complexity and spiritual depth was Jesus of Nazareth.[4] In modern times, however, we owe the idea of individuation primarily to C. G. Jung. The idea originally occurred to Jung when he observed a psychological process taking place in many of his patients and in himself which was not initiated by the concerns of the ego but from a deeper inner center. Jung perceived that in such cases the health of the individual required a concentration upon this process. This process Jung called "individuation" because it seemed to be aiming at the development of a whole, complete, and individual personality. The goal of the individuation process, however, was not by any means necessarily coincident with the stated goals of the ego. In fact, as Fritz Kunkel has shown, the process of individuation is always in opposition to our egocentric goals; it can only be fulfilled when the egocentric ego finally accepts the necessity of subordinating itself to the requirements from the greater Center within, or, to put the matter in religious language, the necessity to acknowledge the higher power of the Will of God.[5]

To think like an ancient Greek and acknowledge the power of Ananke brings about an attitude markedly different from the "get what you want" attitude so prevalent not only in present-day culture as a whole, but even in certain kinds of psychological systems. The message of Ananke, however, is that there is only one freedom: to serve God in whatever way the Deity presents itself to us. Thus, the paradox is that liberation for the ego does not consist in a life led without any restraints or requirements, but comes when we voluntarily accept necessity: the necessities imposed upon us from within and without which life requires from us. For this reason individuation is not a libertarian "do as you please," but is quite the opposite: it means serving the demands of those Higher Powers that human beings have always called God. In this lies the cure. In this regard it is worth noting that the Greek word *therapeuō*, from which we derive our word *therapy*, means not only to heal or cure, but also to "render service to the gods."

Ananke means there are constraints and limits within which we must live. In our present culture we tend to forget that there are legitimate limits which must be observed; the Greeks were very aware of it, for which reason they said that Ananke had a sister goddess—Themis—whose function it was to establish and preside over all the boundaries and limits which we mortals must observe. It is to Themis that we now turn.

Notes

1. Plato 1984e, 195c. "I say he [Eros] is the youngest of the gods and ever young, while those early dealings with the gods which Hesiod and Parmenides relate, I take to have been the work of Necessity and not of Love."
2. See *Antony* in *Plutarch's Lives* (1962), paras. 1, 112.
3. South African Jungian analyst Vera Buhrmann has done a great deal of research into the lore of the Ancestors, who are the "geniuses" for the Amaghirha, the native healers of the Transkei in South Africa. See also Broster 1981.
4. See Sanford 1974 and 1987.
5. See Sanford 1984.

3

$\mathscr{T}$HEMIS AND $\mathscr{H}$ER $\mathscr{D}$AUGHTERS

$\mathscr{O}$ur inner cities seem to be crumbling, as our population shifts from the country to the city, and waves of immigrants reach our shores, heading for the urban centers. Meanwhile, an unprecedented number of children are born out of wedlock, while family life in general is eroded by the complexity of modern life, and in many cases by a large number of children for whom the parent or parents cannot provide. Our prisons are full to capacity; and, as fast as a new prison is built, it too fills up, as an increasing number of people live in disdain of the law and the legal and moral rights of others. With the growing number of broken homes, social pressure, and lack of positive religious influence, more and more people need psychological or psychiatric help, straining society's health facilities to the utmost. The number of people who are out of work makes old-timers think of the Depression in the 1930s, and even among the employed, earnings often seem inadequate to meet the financial demands of a complex society and way of life.

Something seems wrong with our country, but while different people have different opinions, none of them seem to hit the mark. Ancient Greeks, however, would have had an explanation. The problem, they would have said, is that the goddess Themis has been disregarded, and because she has been offended, she exacts payment from a human race which has become so infected with hubris that it now disregards the honor and prerogative of the gods. Who is this Themis who was so important to the Greeks that they would have laid the blame for our society's ills at our disdainful neglect of her rights and requirements?

As we have noted, long before the Olympian deities, with their essentially masculine bias, came on the scene in Greece, the ancient matriarchal order emanated from Gaia—Mother Earth herself. But almost as important as Gaia was the goddess Themis, a deity so old that she was virtually one with the Mother Goddess; indeed, she was called "the spirit and will of Gaia" and was regarded as the embodiment of the justice and the voice of Gaia herself. Long before Apollo took over the oracular seat at Delphi, it belonged to Gaia, but it was Themis who often spoke here on behalf of her mother: "First in this my prayer," says the prophetess at the beginning of Aeschylus' *Eumenides*, "I give the place of chiefest honor among the gods to the first prophet, Earth [Gaia]; and after her to Themis, for she, as it is told, took second this oracular seat of her mother" (1983b, 1–4).

The name Themis comes from the root of the Greek word *tithēmi*, which means to put or place; so Themis refers to all that is put or placed down as right and needful. Themis is, in fact, the goddess of "that which is Right"—not in a moralistic sense, but in the sense of "correct" because it is divinely sanctioned. Hence, she is the guardian of all the boundaries and limits ordained by the gods to be observed by all living creatures: the fish of the sea, the birds of the air, and all creatures who creep, crawl, or walk on the face of the earth, including us human beings. Themis thus presides over what can be called "Right Order"; indeed, this is the meaning of her name. The "Right Order" of Themis begins with the order that prevails in nature, but includes as well all those unwritten but real laws which regulate human life. This order includes the correct relationship that should exist among human beings, between human beings and the natural order, and between mortals and the gods. Thus, Themis ordains all the unwritten but divinely sanctioned laws that regulate the proper relationships of men and women, parents and children, rulers and subjects, as well as the "Right Order" that must prevail in any economic system. Since order always implies limits, Themis is also the goddess of limits and boundaries par excellence.

Greek scholar Jane Harrison has said that Themis began as a personified abstraction, but became in the passage of time a real personality. She notes astutely, "The making of a goddess is always a mystery, the outcome of manifold causes of which we have lost count" (1955, 270). The essence of Themis is further revealed in her three daughters, goddesses who amplify the nature of their mother. First in importance among these was the goddess Dikē, whose name means custom, law, and justice. Completing the triumvirate were Dikē's sisters Eunomia (Good Order) and Eirene (Peace). Dikē is often pictured carrying the sword of justice; when provoked, she could also be the divine agency which wreaked vengeance on those who wantonly disregarded the just will and laws of the gods. In Euripides' play *The Bacchanals* there is a cry for vengeance on King Pentheus for his cruel mistreatment of the women who have chosen to follow the ecstatic god Dionysus. When this happened, Euripides tells us, there was a clamor for Justice:

> Justice [Dikē], draw nigh, with the sword of avenging appear:
> Slay the unrighteous, the seed of Echion [i.e., Pentheus], the earth-born, and shear
> Clean through his throat, for he fearest not God, neither law doth he fear. (1979a, 991ff)

Akin to Dikē as a companion goddess to Themis was the dreaded Nemesis, whose name means "Just Retribution" and "Vengeance." The name "Nemesis" has come down into our English language as a word in its own right; it means "a just punishment" or sometimes the one who imposes such a punishment.[1] Whenever the "Right Order" of Themis was wantonly disregarded, then Dikē or Nemesis was sent to bring justice and to exact vengeance and destruction on the offenders. "When Themis is disregarded, Nemesis is there," comments Professor Kerényi (1951, 102).

The will of Themis also extended to the amount of good fortune and happiness any mortal had the right to expect, for while such well-being was not entirely forbidden to mortals, there was nonetheless a limit to what was considered right in this area. The Greek historian Herodotus cites the story of King

Polycrates as the case of a man who exceeded the amount of good fortune to which any mortal was entitled, and consequently was brought low by Themis and her consort deities Nemesis and Dikē. It seems that everything went just the way King Polycrates wanted it to. First he won a dispute with his two brothers and was able to seize all power for himself. He then made a pact of friendship with Amasis, King of Egypt. Secure that he would not be attacked by Amasis, Polycrates made war on his neighbors and won all his battles. His fleet now had a hundred and fifty galleys and carried a force of a thousand bowmen. His widespread raids brought enormous wealth to his capital and extended his empire far and wide.

His ally Amasis, however, was aware of the dangers that were hidden within Polycrates' very success, and accordingly wrote him a letter as follows:

> Amasis to Polycrates: It is a pleasure to hear of a friend and ally doing well, but, as I know that the gods are jealous of success, I cannot rejoice at your excessive prosperity. My own wish, both for myself and for those I care for, would be to do well in some things and badly in others, passing through life with alternate success and failure; for I have never yet heard of a man who after an unbroken run of luck was not finally brought to complete ruin. Now I suggest that you deal with the danger of your continual successes in the following way: think of whatever it is you value most— whatever you would most regret the loss of—and throw it away; throw it right away, so that nobody can ever see it again. If, after that, you do not find success alternates with failure, then go on using the remedy I have advised. (Herodotus 1990, 3.41)

Polycrates took his ally's advice to heart and pondered what was his most valuable possession. He finally settled on a large emerald ring, set in gold, fashioned by a craftsman with consummate skill. He then manned a galley, went to sea, and cast the ring into the depths of the water while all his entourage watched. Then he returned home, lamenting the loss of his treasure, but confident his action would satisfy the gods' jealousy of human success, and spare him from the wrath of Dikē and vengeance of Nemesis. But, alas! as the gods would have it, a fish swallowed the jewel, a fisherman caught the fish, and since it was such a fine fish brought it to the king as a gift. When the king's servants cut open the fish to cook it for dinner—lo! —there was the ring! Triumphantly the servants returned the precious jewel to the king, of course thinking that he would be greatly pleased; indeed, Polycrates was delighted at this further good fortune, believing it an act of divine providence. But when King Amasis was informed of this, he thought otherwise and declared, "How impossible it is for one man to save another from his destiny," which Amasis now believed would be a miserable death. Just to be on the safe side Amasis wrote Polycrates a letter ending their alliance; he did not want to be associated with Polycrates when the inevitable divine calamity fell upon him lest the gods decide that he too should share Polycrates' fate. So it was that in the end, Polycrates' squadrons revolted against him. He made overtures of friendship to his old enemies the Persians, but the Persian Satrap Oroetes only feigned friendship with him so as to take him captive unaware. Polycrates fell into the trap and died a miserable death by crucifixion.

As we know, many of the older matriarchal deities diminished in importance after the Olympian deities usurped their power, but Themis is an exception. Homer tells us that after the ascendancy of the Olympian deities, Zeus brought Themis to Olympus as well, where she became his advisor, almost like his very thoughts (Homer 1978, 15.88). The Greek poet Pindar tells us that she was even wed to Zeus before Hera became his wife, and through Zeus begat the three Hours, whom we have already had occasion to mention. For whatever reason, when Zeus wished to call an assembly of the gods, it was Themis who began their deliberations with the proper speech, for which reason mortals also invoked Themis whenever they met together for council or deliberations.

For the Greek mind, then, an excess of success and happiness was to be avoided, and if it persisted, one should not draw attention to it. Aeschylus, commenting on the story of Polycrates, said, "Glory in excess is fraught with peril. 'Tis the lofty peak that is smitten with heaven's thunderbolt" (1983a, 468ff). Sophocles also recommended that we mortals should be wary when things are going well for us, even if that good fortune seems to persist into our advanced years. He advised:

Wait to see life's ending e'er thou count a mortal blest;
Wait till free from pain and sorrow he has gained his
final rest. (1962, 235–6)

We may smile at what might appear a quaint attitude about too much success on the part of the classical Greeks, but their ancient warnings live on in our "superstitious" custom of knocking on wood after we verbalize something good that has happened to us. The notion is that the devil might hear what we have said and maliciously wreck things for us; the wood, as previously noted, is the Cross of Christ, an antidote to the devil's evil intentions.

Themis is to be observed in the area of human relationships in particular, for all relationships have certain boundaries and limits within which they thrive. Should these boundaries be disregarded, then an avenging spirit endangers the relationship and may well destroy it. This is a way of saying that every relationship has built into it a "Right Order" or Themis.

Friendship, for instance, is a relationship in which the relational needs of both persons must be met. If the relationship is unbalanced, with one friend deriving significantly more satisfaction from the relationship than the other, then the depth of the friendship will be diminished, or perhaps will not survive at all. It is in the nature of friendship that it also tends to be an "understated" relationship, for friends may be quite devoted to each other but seldom mention it. Yet, friendship is not endangered by this lack of an ostentatious display of affection; it is in the nature of friendship that it thrive on a "low profile," for it is nourished silently from within. This is especially likely to be the way with men who are friends, for men tend naturally to be shy or even embarrassed at too much display of affection. Indeed, too overt a display of affection may make friends uneasy, perhaps because of the fear that a friendship may go "over the line" from friendship into erotic love. At the same time, friendship in which *no* words or sincere gestures of friendship are ever exchanged may be deprived of certain necessary psychological nutrients. Where is the line between "not enough" and "too much"? It is not always easy to discern, but such a line does exist, established by Themis, the "Right Order."

Another boundary that must not be crossed in the relationship between friends involves the Shadow, the name we give to that dark, perhaps even sinister, part of our personality of which we are all too often unaware. The Shadow will likely include our more devious and selfish motives, which are often hidden from others as well as from ourselves. It certainly will include our more egocentric side; to the extent that we are egocentric, we use other people for the benefit of our needs. A friendship cannot survive, though, if too many self-serving egocentric needs intrude into it. This egocentric aspect of our personalities is our "shadow," and it is Themis who prevents the shadow from intruding into our relationships with friends. The shadow may manifest itself in other relationships, but if we inflict our shadow on our friend, then we have "gone over a line," and the friendship will be in jeopardy.

The entrance of an enemy into the relationship is another complicating factor which can destroy a friendship. If two friends have a common enemy, then their friendship is cemented even more closely together. But if one of the friends has a person in his or her life who is seen as an enemy, but the other does not share that enmity, then there is a danger the friendship may weaken. This will certainly be the case if our friend should ever take the side of our enemy in a dispute. Such are the psychological laws and limits which underlie the "Right Order" of friendship and endow it with "Themis."

With lovers, the matter is somewhat different. As we have noted, praise and overt expressions of affection are more natural and allowable in the relationship of lovers than in that of friends. Just as a plant requires water for its life, so the relationship of lovers requires demonstrations of love and affection. As with friends, so with lovers; the shadow must not intrude too much into the relationship, but curiously enough, the relationship of lovers can often stand more of the shadow element than can that of friends, perhaps because it is nourished from diverse sources, or perhaps because Aphrodite herself was known to have a strong shadow element in which she frequently indulged.

Jealousy also constitutes a threat to friendship. If, for instance, one friend achieves a certain measure of success, or has a certain amount of good fortune which the other friend covets, then jealousy may arise. This jealousy will certainly undermine the friendship unless the jealous person works diligently on himself or herself in order to prevent it from interfering. This hard work on the part of the jealous partner to the successful friend is, of course, a sign that the jealous person values the friendship more than the element of success which he or she covets.

In a relationship between lovers, however, jealousy is almost certain to occur. Themis governs this, too, so the relationship of lovers, while disturbed by jealousy, often survives it. Ordinarily, the disturbing factor is jealousy over the affection one's lover shows to someone else, but sometimes jealousy arises over the lover's worldly successes—especially when both partners have similar ambitions. This latter kind of jealousy is often more dangerous to the relationship of lovers than is the jealousy which stems from difficulties in the area of eros, for the latter jealousies are an almost inevitable part of the world of Aphrodite, but the former jealousies lead to the intrusion of egocentric factors into the relationship.

Another area in which Themis is particularly present and important lies in the realm of certain professional relationships such as exist between priests or ministers and their parishioners, between doctors and their patients, and between psychotherapists and their clients. We will take the latter relationship as an example.

The relationship of therapist and client is by nature an intimate one. The client may discuss certain issues with the therapist which are not shared with anyone else. Carefully guarded secrets may be revealed, hidden fantasies shared, and dark corners of the client's life explored. As a result of such intimacy, a close bond may spring up between the therapist and client, consisting of the "transference" which the client makes to the therapist and the "counter-transference" of the therapist to the client. If therapy is to succeed, it is important that the relationship "hold water," that is, confidentiality is maintained, respect is mutual, and powerful personal emotions, should they arise, are not "acted out" but are contained in the crucible of the therapeutic structure. To put the matter in a mythological framework, it is important that Themis be honored in the relationship, that a Right Order prevails; otherwise, the healing energy generated in the relationship leaks out like water from a bottle with holes in it. Thus, while many of the emotional and psychological needs of the client may legitimately be satisfied in the relationship with the therapist, only two of the needs of the therapist can legitimately be satisfied: the financial need and (sometimes) the need to do the work. The therapist's personal emotional needs—perhaps for intimacy, sharing, or adulation—need to be excluded from the professional relationship and find fulfillment in the therapist's personal life. It is particularly important that the sexual needs of the therapist not be indulged with a client, even if the client should appear to encourage them. It is also important that the relationship not be allowed by the therapist to lead to his or her inflation, which is always a possibility if the client makes too much of the therapist. All of this is Themis, the Right Order of the therapeutic relationship "container"; it is the archetypal foundation for the proper work of healing to rest upon.

Themis is also to be found in the social order, for here too there are lines, limits, and boundaries which must exist in a social order if it is to function properly. An obvious example is the penal code. The penal code systematically demarcates the line between acceptable and unacceptable behavior. If, for instance, you drive 65 mph on the freeway in California—even if the speed limit is technically 55 mph—this will ordinarily be regarded as acceptable, and the highway patrol will ignore the technical infraction of the law; but if you should drive 70 or 75 mph, then you have crossed a *de facto* "line," and you may well be stopped by the highway patrol and have to pay a fine. Thus, the highway patrol acts as the guardian of Themis, of what is the Right Order that should prevail on the freeway.

Then there is the matter of the income tax. The Internal Revenue Service guards and enforces the "lines" drawn by the U.S. government, establishing how much should be paid by us in taxes and what sources of money might come to us on which we do not need to pay taxes (such as inheritances up to a certain amount). Nevertheless, there are certain "gray" areas where either legally or morally the matter is not always clear. Let us say that you furnish your office with a computer which, however, you also use occasionally for personal matters. Is it correct or not correct, morally and legally, to disregard the fact that the computer is not always used strictly for business? Or, suppose you find you can avoid paying some taxes by not reporting certain sources of revenue which are readily kept secret? This is a concern of special importance to therapists or other contractors for service who are sometimes paid in cash. Is it in accordance with Themis or not to report such income? The IRS knows what it thinks about it, but what about the individual who knows she or he can "get away with it" but still has to reckon with the matter of conscience? Somewhere in this issue lies the goddess Themis, who presides over a Right Order that transcends the wishes of any particular individual.

Themis is especially to be found in nature; wherever nature is left to herself, the Right Order of Mother Nature prevails. A wilderness area, kept free from the disruptive incursions of human beings, always establishes a Right Order under the guidance of Themis. Let us say that it is spring and you are in the high desert mountain country of the American Southwest. You have hiked far enough into the mountains to be away from cities and farms and roads, and the remoteness of the land you are in leaves it in a pristine condition, much as it must have been centuries ago, before what we call civilization intruded upon the Themis of Mother Nature. Here in the springtime of these mountains the desert is bursting forth. Birds have returned from their winter refuges, and their mating songs fill the air with life. Cactus is beginning to explode with its brilliant red or yellow flowers. Wind moves gently but pervasively over the land, distributing the seeds of new life everywhere. Plant roots go down deep into the ground, searching for water that springtime rains have sent seeping into the earth. Coyotes are about at dusk seeking rabbits and mice, which in turn defend their existence by ancient systems for concealing themselves, and by producing such a prodigious number of offspring that their survival as a species is guaranteed.

Hiking through this terrain you can feel your heart rejoice, and you feel strangely at one with a marvelous landscape over which members of your race have walked for thousands of years. All of this is Themis. Yet, there is also a dark side to this world. Poisonous snakes crawl about, enjoying the warm air after their long winter hibernation; their territory and rights must be respected, for they are ignored only at your peril. You must also be aware all the time of just where you are in this strange landscape, and aware also of the passage of the sun through the sky; if you get lost, and darkness and cold descend upon you, it will go hard with you. All of this is also Themis, the Right Order of the primordial landscape in which you find yourself.

Themis also sees that the population of a species not exceed its proper limits. When the population of any given species exceeds its proper number, then that population is typically reduced by disease or by the increase of the predators which, by means of preying upon the excess population, keep the species within certain bounds. When the Right Order of population cannot be controlled by nature, then a breakdown appears to occur in the social instincts of the animals involved. An experiment that took place in the 1950s illustrates this. In this experiment, a modest number of rats were placed in a confined area. There was ample room for the rats, and sufficient food and water was provided. The observers noted that the rats quickly established a viable social order and lived together in harmony. Then the experimenters gradually introduced more rats into the same living space; at the same time they also provided more food and water so that there was enough of both to go around. Despite there being a sufficiency of food and water for all, it was noted that as the rat population increased but their living area did not, social tension began to mount. Eventually the rats began to fight with each other, and after a certain "line" had been crossed in the increasing population, the rats began to turn on each other viciously. It seems clear that for Themis—"Right Order"—to be present among the rats, a certain amount of space had to be provided for.

Does this also apply to human beings? In our crowded cities and countries, has the "Right Order" been disregarded? Has there been a "going over the line" of Themis with respect to the number of human beings who can live together in a given space and still have a viable social order? Is our high crime rate and increasing disregard for the rights of our neighbors at least partly the result of the disregard of "Right Order" in this respect? If so, then Themis will send some kind of destruction to try to correct the disorder.

The importance of Themis and the boundaries and limits she imposes on people are also manifested clinically. Alcoholism and drug addiction, for instance, are psychiatric and spiritual

45

disorders in which the individual does not or cannot establish limits on the intake of addictive substances. Certain people can consume alcohol in moderate quantities—thus observing Themis—but others cannot. Programs such as Alcoholics Anonymous help these people find the rule of Themis in their lives, and this enables them to control their consumption of alcohol.

The inability of certain people to regulate properly the ebb and flow of money is another symptom of the inability, or lack of desire, to observe the "Right Order" of money. In fact, it could be said that the inability to observe the Themis of economics and financial matters is a disease which infects virtually our whole nation from the government on down. Because the reckless spending and borrowing of money comes from "on high," from the government itself, it is not often recognized in individuals to be the serious psychological and spiritual disorder which it is— a disorder springing from the disregard of Themis in relationship to money.

Themis also is built into our psychic energy systems. For instance, a certain amount of depression or "low spirits" is natural for us, as are times when our spirits are high. For some people, however, the low spirits seem to have no bottom to them; the mood then goes down and down to create a clinical depression. Similarly, the "highs" may not have a natural ceiling to them, resulting in a euphoria or mania. The situation is like an elevator which gets to the top of the building, but instead of stopping, keeps on going up into the sky, and when it finally does descend, it is unable to "bottom out." The result is the psychiatric condition of manic-depressive illness, in which the body's natural mood-regulating function is not working. Fortunately, this lack can usually be compensated for by the judicial use of lithium and anti-depressive drugs. With this help Themis is reestablished with regard to the movement of psychic energy within an individual personality.

The ancient Chinese book of Taoist wisdom, the *I Ching* (Book of Changes) has an instruction section on the matter of Themis; in fact, the hexagram in question (No. 60) is entitled *CHIEH* which means "Limitation." The image on which the meditative thoughts of this hexagram are based is that of a lake. A lake, the *I Ching* observes, occupies a contained space; thus, the lake sets limits for the water which it holds. If the allowable

amount of water in the lake is exceeded, then the water over-
flows. In this way the lake retains its integrity. Commentator
Richard Wilhelm points out that the Chinese word for limitation
is the same as the word which refers to the joints that divide a
bamboo stalk into its different sections, yet hold the bamboo
stalk together. These dividing lines on the bamboo stalk, Wilhelm suggests, represent the limits imposed on all human activ-
ity; the hexagram particularly applies to the limits that must be
set on expenditures of money and energy, and on the fixed limits that the "superior man" will set on his actions. Wilhelm further observes:

> A lake is something contained. Water is inexhaustible. A
> lake can contain only a definite amount of the infinite quan-
> tity of water; this is its peculiarity. In human life too the
> individual achieves significance through discrimination
> and the setting of limits. Therefore what concerns us here is
> the problem of clearly defining these discriminations,
> which are, so to speak, the backbone of morality. Unlimited
> possibilities are not suited to man; if they existed, his life
> would only dissolve in the boundless. To become strong, a
> man's life needs the limitations ordained by duty and vol-
> untarily accepted. The individual attains significance as a
> free spirit only by surrounding himself with these limita-
> tions and by determining for himself what his duty is. (Wil-
> helm 1950, 247)

There is also, however, a "limit on limit," for when there
are too many limitations on a person, limitations which do not
spring from necessity for a correctly lived life, then these are
galling. "Therefore," Wilhelm concludes his commentary on the
I Ching, "it is necessary to set limits even upon limitation" (1950,
247). Psychologically, an example of this lies in the way in which
human sexual energy is expended. The old Victorian ideal may
well have represented "galling limitation," a limitation that was
too constricting, and which resulted in the typical neuroses
which engendered psychoanalysis at the turn of this century. On
the other hand, our present sexual mores, such as they are, provide little if any container for our sexual energy, and so they go
too far in the other direction. Somewhere in the middle lies
"Themis"—the Right Order of sexual instinct.

Clearly it is in our best interests, as the Greeks perceived, to heed the Will of God and follow the ways of Themis; then both our personal life and our life as a society will proceed correctly and be supported by divine favor. But it is also clear that all too often human beings disregard the boundaries established by Themis. Why do we mortals persist in following life-patterns that are clearly against our self-interest? The answer, the Greeks suggested, lies with still another goddess: the dread goddess Atē, to whom we now turn.

Note

1. *Webster's New World Dictionary.*

4

$\mathcal{F}$OLLY, $\mathcal{R}$UIN, AND $\mathcal{S}$IN:

THE GODDESS ATĒ

$\mathcal{I}$n our present century we have reached a new height in civilization. Medical science has grown by leaps and bounds. A wonderful new technology has transformed the world and made life easier. Human skill and ingenuity have produced one marvelous invention after another. But it also must be said that this century has produced a multitude of horrors which rivals or exceeds anything known in our history. A succession of senseless wars have involved almost the entire world, each one having been more ferocious and inhuman than its predecessor. Not only have combatants been maimed or killed, but women and children have also been bombed, gassed, and shot. At this present time the world is, fortunately, relatively peaceful, except of course for the inevitable "little wars" in which certain smaller countries are presently, and apparently chronically, engaged.

Moreover, what has come on the heels of war is not exactly worthy of the name of peace; there now exists a rate of crime, brutality, social disintegration, and corruption in high places so great that it staggers the imagination. It is as though a deep pathology in human nature which once was expressed through war is now turned inward against society itself. Even a casual reading of the daily newspaper or listening to the news on television is enough to make any thoughtful person ask: What kind of people are we anyway? Is there a deadly madness that possesses the human race? What is this hidden power in us which destroys or warps our social conscience and blunts our human sensibilities to the sufferings of others? Is our will free to choose the good, or is the will helplessly in the grip of evil?

At one time people looked to myth and religion to answer these questions, but today we are trained to look to science for rational answers. The science of human behavior is psychology, but psychology does not seem to be of much help when it comes to answering the question of the origins of human evil. The recently published and voluminous *Concise Encyclopedia of Psychology* (John Wiley and Sons, 1987) does not even have a heading on evil. From this omission I suppose we must conclude that there is no evil, or if there is, it is not deemed worthy of psychological discussion. As for sin, it also must either not exist or not be deemed important, since the only article in the encyclopedia on that subject is a brief one discussing such things as the difference between mortal and venial sin. Lacking a viable concept of sin, we are left with more rational explanations for the existence of human evil, such as the idea that people act in an evil way because of bad parenting or unfavorable social conditions. The idea seems to be that if only there were a world in which all parents were kind and enlightened people, and all social orders were perfect, then human evil would cease to exist.

Where science fails in dealing with such fundamental existential questions, we do well to turn to mythology, for mythology embodies within it the deep archetypal patterns which influence both individual human behavior and the social order. This being so, it is not surprising to find that from the dawn of history, human beings have been aware of evil conditions similar to those we lament today, and that all over the world they tried to account for the existence of human evil through stories that emanate from the unconscious collective psyche, those stories that we call myths.

Among the Nez Percé Indians, for instance, we find the interesting and instructive story of Cannibal.[1] To summarize the tale: it seems five brothers went hunting, but only four returned home; Elder Brother did not come back. The people began to worry, so Coyote sent out the second brother to look for him. He found Elder Brother; but, alas! Elder Brother was hideous to look at. He had no flesh on him, for he had eaten himself. Elder

Brother then lassoed Second Brother and ate him up also. The same fate awaited the third brother and also the fourth. Finally only Younger Brother was left, and Coyote reluctantly sent him as well to find out what had happened. But Younger Brother came across Meadowlark on the way, and Meadowlark helped Younger Brother by telling him what to do. With the help of Meadowlark's advice, Younger Brother found out what had happened to his brothers and was able to escape Cannibal's lasso and find his way home. Coyote declared that Elder Brother had indeed become self-eaten and that the People must flee. Eventually Cannibal was killed by Crane in the following way: Crane asked to be buried with only his legs protruding. When Cannibal came up to him to investigate, Crane quickly pulled his legs out and kicked Cannibal so hard that all his bones came rattling down. Crane ran home with the news, "Now I killed him. Now we are free." From that time on there was peace.

This instructive myth tells us many things about evil. First, its origin is irrational; there is no explanation given in the story for Elder Brother's behavior. Second, evil cannot exist on its own, for Cannibal is self-eaten; he has devoured his own energy and can now live only on the energy of others. This tells us evil cannot create; it only lives if there is something good and sound for it to destroy. It is like a virus, which cannot survive on its own but must dwell within a more or less healthy body in order to exist.

Other cultures had other stories to account for evil; each of them is instructive in its own way. The ancient Hebrews said that God so despaired of the human race—because of human beings' constant wicked schemes—that he regretted having made them and decided to drown them all in a great flood. He decided to spare only Noah and his family, for Noah alone was a righteous and upright man. God bade Noah build an Ark and put his wife, his two sons, and a pair of all the animals on the Ark. Then, the flood came, and wicked humanity was drowned. But that was not the end of the matter. After the flood was over, and Noah and all the animals were safely on dry land again, God made the curious statement: "Never again will I curse the earth because of human beings, because their heart contrives evil from their infancy. Never again will I strike down every living thing as I have done." God, it seems, discovered that not

51

even his radical solution of sending the flood would prevent a renewed human race from plotting and engaging in evil.

Evil in this story is like a weed which springs up in a beautiful garden, seemingly from nowhere, and destroys the good and desirable plants. And so it seems to be. Just as a good gardener pulls up the weeds so the flowers and vegetables can grow, so society tries to root out evil. Just as the weeds in a garden always spring up again even after the gardener has carefully pulled them out, so too evil springs up ever anew, for the seeds of the weeds of evil seem to come from a deep source in the human psyche. The battle to keep evil from taking over completely is as never-ending as the battle the gardener wages against the invasive weeds.

Now the Greeks also had a story to account for evil. Evil, they said, entered the human heart through the power of the goddess Atē, and through that "original sin" of the human race which the Greeks called *hubris*, of which we will have more to say shortly. We have seen that most of the goddesses had a dark side and could be destructive to mortals under certain conditions, especially if they were ignored, but they were not intent on evil for its own sake, and they had a positive side as well. The goddess Atē, however, was simply bent on spreading folly, ruin, and sin amongst humankind just for the hell of it. So malevolent was she that it is hard to find even one good thing to say about her, yet we ignore Atē at our own peril. Better is it to live in constant awareness of her reality and of her power to bring ruin to our lives, than to delude ourselves by saying she does not exist.

Atē was said to have Zeus for her father and the goddess Eris for her mother. Now Eris is the goddess of strife, and Zeus is the god of power, and it seems that Atē combined in herself the willfulness of her father and the quarrelsomeness of her mother; it is she who leads human beings into willful strife and foolish confusion. Indeed, the Greek word *atē* means "bewilderment, infatuation, and reckless impulse."[2] Atē is that deity who, when she has possessed or deceived a mortal, causes that person to lose all powers of moral discrimination, capacity for sound judgment, or even ability to act out of enlightened self-interest. Hers is such a diabolical nature that she was consistently referred to by Aeschylus as "treacherous Atē" (cf. Aeschylus 1983a, 1230).

Thus, according to the Greeks, Atē instills in human hearts a wanton disregard for both morals and for the consequences of our actions. It is she who confuses our minds and so blinds us spiritually that we not only act with a disregard for what is morally right but also for our own long-term self-interest. Bewildered by the reckless impulses Atē instills in us, we human beings are led to our ultimate ruin. Small wonder that Atē, along with Ares, the god of war, was the most hated of all the deities; yet mortals find they are fatally attracted to her nonetheless, though she leads them inexorably to a dark fate.

All of this discussion of Atē could be dismissed as the product of a fanciful imagination except that even a casual reading of the morning newspaper reveals that everything Atē personifies is alive and well today. All the way from the fiscal policies of our government to the high incidence of crime in our cities and the way we are despoiling our natural resources is a testimony to the psychological and spiritual reality of a spiritual force or power which leads to our destruction.

Atē did not always live on earth; at one time, we are told, her home was on Mt. Olympus with the other gods. It seems she was able to scramble and delude their divine wits with almost as much ease as she scrambled the wits of mortals. The story of how Atē was eventually expelled from Olympus and came to live on earth has to do with her going one step too far in her meddling in the affairs of Zeus, a story that Homer tells us in the *Iliad* (1978, 87–137).

The story begins with the pregnancies of two women. One of them, Alcmene by name, was the favorite of Zeus. The other, Eileithyia, was the favorite of Zeus's wife Hera. Zeus was determined that the son born of his favorite Alcmene would be selected to become the lord of the people on earth when he grew to manhood, but Hera was equally determined that Eileithyia's child should have this honor, and the power and influence that went with it. Hera's determination was fueled not only because Eileithyia was her favorite, but also because she was jealous of the special relationship which Zeus had with Alcmene. Zeus, of course, had ultimate power when it came to heavenly decisions, but Hera was not without her own resources. She came up with a scheme to ensure that her favorite won the prize. Using all of her wiles, she proposed to Zeus that the child of whichever of the two women gave birth first should rule the world of human beings. Zeus was suspicious of Hera's proposal, having prior experience of her scheming ways, but he was also aware that Alcmene was much further along in her pregnancy than Eileithyia. For this reason it seemed certain to Zeus that the child of his favorite would be born first. Nevertheless, Zeus's suspicions persisted. Even though he did not see any way that Alcmene's child would not be born first, he was still not ready to agree to Hera's bargain because of his natural good sense and caution.

At this point Atē entered the scene. Atē so blinded the eyes of Zeus and so confused his mind that the latter was eventually persuaded to agree to Hera's plan and even to take a mighty oath that the firstborn child should rule the world of mortals. Once Zeus's oath was taken—and not even a god could break such an oath—Hera then magically delayed the birth of Alcmene's son and hastened the birth of Eileithyia's. Now, Alcmene's son was none other than the future hero Heracles, and Eileithyia's son was the ordinary mortal Eurystheus. So it was that when the two babes were born, Heracles, despite being Zeus's favorite, had to serve Eurystheus throughout his lifetime.

When Zeus realized how he had allowed himself to be tricked, he was furious at Atē; he knew that he had made his foolish decision only because Atē had blinded his mind and ruined his powers of good judgment. He was so furious at Atē that he snatched her up, whirled her round and round, and threw her with all his might out of heavenly Olympus. Down, down Atē fell until she finally landed—where else?—on earth. Ever since, Atē has wandered the world, inciting human beings to acts of folly, ruin, and sin by destroying their good judgment, confusing their minds, and obliterating their moral sensibilities. So destructive was her influence and so prevalent her presence on earth, that earth itself was called by the ancients "the meadow of Atē."

To make matters worse, it was also said of Atē that she never walked on the ground; instead she walked on the heads of mortals, leaping from one head to another as she made her way around the world. This she did because her feet were exquisitely dainty, and she did not want them defiled by the rough earth. "Delicate are her feet," Homer relates, "for on the ground she speeds not, only on the heads of men" (Homer 1978,

19.92ff; cf. Plato 1984e, 195D). What the effect of this was on us mortals we are not told, but we can be sure that having Atē leap from head to head did not do us any good.

Once people were influenced by Atē, they had no recourse except to appeal at once for the prayers of the three Litae. The Litae, whose name means "prayers" and from which name we derive our ecclesiastical word *litany*, were the helpers of humanity. Aware of the trouble Atē caused, and filled with compassion for hapless and witless mortals, they followed Atē around and offered to help those whom she had afflicted by sending prayers to heaven on their behalf. If a person whose mind and powers of judgment were being influenced by Atē resorted quickly to the Litae and asked for their prayers to the gods above, then the effects of Atē might be averted. But, alas! few mortals recognized their danger in time; consequently, most were impelled to a course of action which led to their destruction.[3]

While the usual source of *atē* was the goddess Atē, in some cases *atē* was sent into human hearts by other deities as well. The Litae, for instance, instead of freeing people from the effects of Atē, sometimes brought *atē* upon them instead. This happened when people ignored the Litae, for to ignore the Litae was in effect to ignore Heaven itself. For instance, the old horseman Phoenix, a man of peace who raised Achilles from childhood and later tried to reconcile Achilles and Agamemnon to help them avert the consequences of their bitter quarrel, noted that Achilles, because of his warlike spirit, was ignoring the Litae. This was tantamount to ignoring the will of Zeus. Phoenix explained the danger Achilles put himself in because of his errant attitude by saying:

> Now whoso revereth the daughters of Zeus (that is, the Litae) when they draw nigh, him they greatly bless, and they hear him when he prays; but if a man denies them and stubbornly refuses, then they go their way and make their prayer to Zeus, the son of Cronos, that Atē may follow after such a one, to the end that he may fall and pay full atonement. (Homer 1978, 9.510ff)

Certain deities were especially likely to be offended by the acts of human beings who were under the baleful influence of

Atē. Among them were the Erinyes (Furies), dread deities of divine vengeance whom we will consider in more detail a little later. Suffice it for now to say that if a person was under the influence of Atē and committed an act which the Erinyes deemed despicable—such as neglecting the laws of relationships and familial duty which these goddesses jealously guarded and enforced—then the Erinyes would virtually guarantee that person's torment and ultimate destruction. Aphrodite was especially likely to send *atē* into the heart of a man or woman afflicted with her erotic passion. Aphrodite, for instance, so afflicted Helen of Troy with *atē* that Helen forsook her own land and husband in a mad passion and fled with Paris to Troy, an event which led (with some more help from Atē) to the disastrous Trojan War. Later, after Helen saw the trouble her actions had brought upon her people, she lamented, "I groaned for the blindness (*atē*) which Aphrodite gave me, when she led me thither from my dear land, forsaking my child and my bridal chamber and my husband, a man who lacked nothing, whether in wisdom or comeliness" (Homer 1978, 4.290ff).

Thus, the erotic passion that Aphrodite could instill in man or woman readily brought *atē* with it, inspiring a lover to reckless actions which ultimately could lead to his or her destruction. So, we read in Euripides' play *Hippolytus* the lament of Phaedra to her nurse because her love-stricken soul's infatuation for the youth Hippolytus caused her such humiliation and pain. She cries out to her companion:

> O hapless I—what is this I have done?
> Witherward have I wandered from wisdom's way?
> I was made, by a God's curse [*atē*] overthrown.
> Oh ill-starred—well-a-day!
> Dear Nurse, veil over mine head once more;
> For I blush for the words from my lips that came.
> Veil me: the tears from mine eyes downpour,
> And mine eyelids sink for shame.
> For anguish awakens when re-dawneth the mind:
> Though a curse be madness, herein is it kind,
> That the soul that it ruins it striketh blind.[4]

In many stories dealing with *atē* we find that a fatal inclination toward *atē* was able to possess a person because that person had succumbed to the sin of *hubris*, one of many Greek words for sin.[5] The sin of hubris is so important that it has come into the English language intact and can be found in most standard dictionaries of the English language, where it is defined as an exaggerated arrogance provoked by excessive pride. To the Greeks, it denoted a wanton violence and insolence—characteristics of what we would call an inflated ego—resulting in a disdainful arrogance which causes a person to despise the laws of the state and the moral imperatives of God. The connection between hubris and *atē* was a favorite theme of Aeschylus, who in his play *Agamemnon* once noted that "Hubris brings Atē into a man's life with her black curses" (1983a, 770).

The goddess Atē could inflict *atē* on a whole nation as well as on individual people. The most famous example is the story of the origin of the war between the Greeks and the Trojans. It all began at the wedding between Peleus and the sea nymph Thetis. Zeus invited all of the gods to this festive occasion except for the goddess Atē. Atē, however, came to the wedding anyway, uninvited, and brought with her a beautiful golden apple: the Golden Apple of Discord. Just for the hell of it, and to express her pique at not being invited to the wedding, she rolled this remarkable golden apple along the banquet table, after having inscribed on it, "For the fairest." As Atē had intended, this stirred up a bitter quarrel among Hera, Athena, and Aphrodite about who was the fairest. To settle the dispute, the handsome young shepherd, Paris, reputed to be especially adroit in matters of love, was asked to judge which of the three goddesses was most beautiful. Paris awarded the prize to Aphrodite, but with Atē continuing to stir up discord, this decision only served to divide the followers of the goddesses into separate warring camps, out of which discord emerged the long and disastrous Trojan War.

In her book *The March of Folly* (1948), historian Barbara Tuchman argued that as with the ancient Greeks and Trojans so with us today; whole nations may be so infected with *atē* that they become involved in foolish courses of action which lead them inevitably to their harm or ruin. Tuchman cites three examples (out of the many she could have chosen) of how a people and nation engaged in a course of action in which folly was matched only by the powers of self-destruction. The first

57

example is how the Papacy during the Renaissance quite unnecessarily provoked the Protestant Secession. Her second example is how King George III of England pursued a wantonly foolish policy toward the American colonies which led, also quite unnecessarily, to the American Revolution and the loss of the colonies. The third example is a modern one: the foolish and ruinous policy of the United States as it pursued its self-destructive course of action in Vietnam.

A study of the goddess Atē and the quality of *atē* which she instills in mortals bring us face-to-face with that vexing question philosophers have long asked: Is the human will free to choose its course of action, or are what appear our choices in fact dictated to us by powers within us and beyond our control? Is the freedom of the will fact or illusion? We have touched on this question before, but now we must explore it more deeply in the light of both the ancient Greek point of view and the findings of contemporary psychology.

As we have noted, the Greek point of view was that we human beings do not exactly decide on a course of action; rather, some deity puts it into our minds or hearts to do it. In our culture, however, we are led to believe that we make decisions on an ego level, that we actively choose whatever action it is in which we engage. We are sure that we are far more enlightened and sophisticated than the Greeks and suppose the Greek point of view—that the gods are behind our actions—is at best quaint and is certainly not to be taken seriously. However, to those acquainted with the psychology of the unconscious, these old stories are psychologically accurate descriptions of how the human mind works, provided that we understand the deities of old to be mythological expressions of the archetypes of the collective unconscious. Understood as the archetypes, Greek deities, and how they affect human thoughts, emotions, and behavior, are profound and accurate statements about how the human mind works, and how, for better or for worse, we are steadily driven and possessed by the power, energy, and seduction of the archetypes. As we have seen, underlying many human actions are primordial patterns of behavior from which emanate the fantasies, fascinations, and inspirations to action which govern all typical transitions and experiences in life. While the archetypes are often helpful to us, perhaps inspiring us to acts of courage or giving us the vital energy with which to carry out our functions as mothers and fathers, doctors or statesmen, workmen or scholars, as often as not they can be ambiguous or even destructive in their effects.

The psychological error that we make today is to think that *we*, on an ego level, think or dream up our ideas and our urges toward action. Let us take, for instance, the emotion of being in love. When we are "in love" and our minds are flooded with images of the beloved and we have all kinds of erotic fantasies, are we really to suppose that *we* are thinking up such things? Or even that the object of our affections is producing such energy? The Greeks would have said that, however attractive the object of our affections might appear to be to us, the fantasies, urges, and sexual arousal which accompany the fantasies of love were manifestations of a deity, in this case Aphrodite, or perhaps her son Eros. The modern point of view regards this as nonsense: there is no deity called Aphrodite and never was; she is a figment of an errant imagination, or at best, a poetic personification of love. But, from the point of view of psychology, the ancient outlook is closer to the truth than the modern. There may not literally be a goddess on Mt. Olympus who floods our minds with images and our hearts with emotions, but the archetype of love and lovemaking is deeply engraved in the very structure of our psyches and does exactly that. Call it by what name we will—god or archetype—the effect is the same.

Or, let us take the phenomenon of war. What produces the psychic energy in humankind that has made us the perpetrators and victims of almost constant warfare throughout our known history? Historians, of course, look for the causes of war in this or that border dispute, or a desire for economic aggrandizement, or some other rational reason. Such issues do play their role, but underlying all of this is the god of war himself, Ares; that is, an archetype for war is embedded in the psyche, which is why, in spite of our protests to the contrary, many of us are fascinated by war. Indeed, some people, such as General Patton of World War Two fame, have the honesty to admit openly that this is the case with them. (He was sorry when it ended and was all for immediately invading the Soviet Union.) Until we face psychological reality and see that there is, indeed, within us mortals something like a god who wants war, we will have little chance of dealing creatively with that energy for war which, in spite of the fact we regard ourselves as civilized, has produced in our century as many or more wars than ever before in history. Given the enormous destructive powers of modern weapons, the luxury of indulging in our psychological ignorance is no longer something we can afford.

Akin to wars which take place between whole nations, there are murders and shootings. Why are murders so prevalent today? Why are there so many guns and why do they seem to be fired so readily? What is the source of the fascination guns hold for people, especially for the male of the species? An interesting saying among the Greeks throws some light on this. First, it must be noted that the Greek word for a weapon was the word for iron, because their weapons were made out of iron. The saying went, "Of itself does the iron draw a man to it" (Homer 1984, 16.294). The meaning is this: that a weapon exerts a certain fascination upon a man's mind. The gun draws a person into its sphere of influence by conjuring up fantasies about its use. We think that we control the gun; through the fantasies the gun arouses in us, however, the gun exerts control over us. Inevitably, to have a gun is to engender fantasies about using it. Strong-minded and relatively moral people may be equipped to resist these fantasies; those of a weaker mind or those under the influence of certain drugs, or people possessed by a passion of one sort or another, will not always be able to resist, and then the gun *will be used*.

Fortunately, the gods (read archetypes) can be positive and creative as well as destructive. Take music, for example. Many of us have little or no talent or capacity for music; others become great composers, singers, or instrumentalists. With certain musicians such as Mozart, the desire and ability to create music come at an extraordinarily early age. But famous composers like Mozart do not exactly "think up" their music; rather, it is given to them by some source within themselves. Neither do great instrumentalists acquire their talent from the ego, but from a deeper source within themselves—from, the Greeks would say, "the Muse" from whose name our word *music* is derived. Plato wrote about what he called "divine madness." One kind of divine madness, said the great master, came from the Muses. This form of madness "takes hold upon a gentle and pure soul, arouses it and inspires it to songs and other poetry, and thus by adorning countless deeds of the ancients educates later generations." As the bard said in the *Odyssey*, "No teachers have I had; it is the god who implanted the riches of song in my heart" (Homer 1984, 22.347).

Consider why a person becomes a thief. Our modern view suggests that, perhaps, the person was mistreated as a child, and thieving is how he or she expresses anger and frustration; or, perhaps it is because some people are so impoverished that they feel they must steal or are raised with a strong social resentment because they were born into poverty. In many cases factors such as these are important influences. Just the same, many people steal who were not mistreated or socially disadvantaged, and a good many people steal who are not poor but wealthy. In the latter cases, the ways of stealing from others are only more sophisticated; instead of breaking into houses, they may illegally manipulate the financial market or find other highly sophisticated ways of effectually robbing others of their assets.

Thieves who steal by manipulation are called in Greek *kleptēs*; those who rob people by violence are called *lūstēs*. An example of the latter is found in the New Testament story of the man who, having fallen among thieves who beat him and robbed him, was helped by the Good Samaritan (Luke 10:30–37). This kind of thief, so it was said, has a bit of Ares in him, which is why he commits violent crimes. Hermes also included a bit of theft among his many functions, but he was the god of thieves who stole by their wits rather than by violence. Many people steal not because they need something, but because they *are* thieves; and they are thieves because a power within them inspires in them the urge to steal, and "the goddess Atē" blinds them to its consequences.

We "modern" people, of course, suppose that we know better; we rest secure in our belief that there are no gods and, therefore, no obstacles to our adopting rational behavior. But what if the archetype of the thief exists in some people, as an inner autonomous power so strong that it shapes a person's behavior and floods the mind with fantasies of stealing? One family with whose permission I tell this story had several children. They all grew up to be honest and upstanding people, except for one son who at quite an early age began to steal. He would steal from anyone, including his friends, his own family, and friends of the family. Nothing—not his parents, counselors, ministers, or the authorities—could dissuade him from this course of action. It was not surprising then that when he became an adult and continued to steal, he soon found himself in prison for his crimes.

Given the favorable social conditions in which the youth was raised, and the fact that his parents were diligent in their parental duties and gave ample love and security to all their children, it seems hard to account for the way the boy's life turned out. The mother, however, recalled a nightmare which came to her son at about the age of eight, and which so terrified the boy that he ran to awaken his mother and tell her the dream. In this dream the boy was alone in his room when through an open window flew a thief who *entered into him*. From that night, the boy began to steal.

An ancient Greek would have said of such a dream that the god Hermes came into the boy's heart, and since Hermes was, among other things, the god of thieves, it is not surprising that the boy became a thief. The modern rationalist would dismiss such a dream, along with its occurrence at the beginning of the boy's life as a thief, as a mere coincidence. But to one who knows of the reality of the archetypes, it is clear that at the time of the dream, the archetype of the thief was constellated in this boy and possessed him so much that he was inexorably drawn into his life of crime.

Now war leads to ruin, and crimes also lead to ruin; the evidence of such ruin is all around us. Yet, human beings continue to engage in such activities. The Greeks, as we have seen, would have said that this is *atē* and that behind *atē* is the goddess Atē herself, or some like deity who could be equally malevolent. In modern language this is a way of saying that an innate capacity for self-delusion and self-destruction is built into the human psyche. If this be so, then what happens to the notion that human beings have the capacity for something called "free will"? Is the will free to choose its course of action, when so many of our fantasies and thoughts come from powers beyond our control? And if the will is not free, then what does this do to our ideas of right and wrong, and of sin, and of human responsibility for our actions?

Among the later Greek philosophers, the issue of free will

had its supporters and detractors, just as it has had throughout Western philosophy and theology. The Stoics, for instance, opposed the idea of free will, as did the philosopher Democritus. The Pythagoreans, Socrates, Plato, and Epicurus generally favored the idea—as did Aristotle, despite his being something of a philosophical determinist. Virtually all of them agreed, however, that the will was not free to choose without a knowledge of the good, and that ignorance was almost certain to lead to evil.

In contrast, when it comes to the earliest Greek beliefs, there is the widespread opinion that the issue of free will simply never arose. E. R. Dodds, for instance, writes:

> To ask whether Homer's people are determinists (who deny free will) or libertarians (who say we have free will) is a fantastic anachronism: the question never occurred to them, and if it were put to them, it would be very difficult to make them understand what it meant. What they do recognize is the distinction between normal actions and actions performed in a state of *atē*. (1957, 17)

In discussing this issue, Walter F. Otto argues that it is virtually impossible to distinguish between the will of a human being and the power of a deity in Greek thought: "What a man wills and does is himself and is the deity. Both are true, and in the last analysis the same" (Otto 1981, 184). This is true whether the acts and inspirations are positive and helpful, such as the imagination and impulse to make music, or destructive, such as the impulse to war or to commit crimes. Always the same truth is affirmed by the Greeks: if a person has acted in any distinctive way, then somewhere or other a deity has willed it. Paradoxically, even if a god put it into a person's heart to commit an action which was destructive or evil, the person who committed the act is held responsible for his or her sins and merits punishment from Themis, Dikē, and the other deities responsible for avenging infractions of divine law.

This attitude will almost certainly strike us as unreasonable. If a power as awesome as the power of a deity enters into our minds and hearts, and urges us toward a sinful or ruinous course of action, then in what sense can we be held responsible for what we did? The answer has to do with what the Greeks called "the spiritual eye." Through his or her spiritual eye, a person can see what is happening; in this way, people can become aware of the influence of a god upon them. They can also discern the consequences of their actions. But for the spiritual eye to be effective, a person must also have seen those three great Greek realities: the nature of the beautiful, the just, and the reasonable. If a person can develop and hold what we would call in psychology a capacity for conscious insight, for true values, and for "Right Order," then that person need not be so possessed, even by the will of a god, that they are driven to acts of sin or destruction.

Thus, for the Greeks, the idea of what we would call an operative conscience on the one hand and the idea of spiritual and psychological awareness on the other, belong together. This is exemplified in the underlying meaning of the Greek word for conscience, the word *suneidesis*. This word means both "self-awareness," in the sense of knowing what is transpiring within one's mind and heart, and "conscience," that is, an awareness of what is morally correct.[6]

Psychological or spiritual therapy must include the development of *suneidesis*—the capacity for consciousness and spiritual perception. For this reason the Greeks said that if a deity wished to influence a person toward a certain action, one which may run counter to that person's best interests or sense of what is right, then that deity must first confuse the person's mind by "darkening the spiritual eye." As we have seen, the qualities which would so cloud over a person's "spiritual eye" were hubris and *atē*; and the deity most adept at bringing about a person's ruin through the darkening of the spiritual eye by *atē* was the goddess Atē herself. Walter F. Otto summarizes the matter nicely. Referring to the idea that the gods can possess and influence a person's mind and heart, he says:

> It is evident that this conception, closely as it binds man to deity, does not signify that he actually lacks freedom. The impression of constraint is all the more ruled out as man's action is predominantly related to the state of his insight. No external will or desire took possession of him when he chose the worse course, nor was it that his nobler feeling proved powerless in the face of his cruder inclinations. It is only that his clear perception of the beautiful, the just, and

the reasonable—three great realities—was confounded . . .
The mysterious darkening of the spiritual eye is [thus] the
means through which the deity leads to his ruin a man destined to fall. (1981, 185)

Let us conclude this examination of the wellsprings of
humans and the matter of free will by presenting the issue in
psychological language. While the Greeks would say that a god
put it into our minds or hearts to act in a certain way, we would
say that the fantasy leading up to that action and the impulse
toward that action which would follow from the fantasy came
from an archetype. Such an action, of course, might be good and
creative and courageous, but it might also be destructive and
evil. If the ego of a person is stirred up or "infected" by an archetype, then that archetype will possess that person and impel that
person toward a certain typical course of action. If, of course, the
archetype produces an energy which moves toward a worthy or
at least innocuous goal, then well and good, but if the archetype
is destructive, then the results can be malignant. To the extent
that the ego is blind to the profound unconscious spiritual influences at work in his or her psyche (that is, lacking a "spiritual
eye"), then there is effectively little or no free will, but if a person has at least a modicum of psychological insight and spiritual awareness and some warm connections to other human
beings, then the capacity to choose one's actions is still possible.

To develop this kind of consciousness, this "spiritual eye,"
it is helpful to develop what can be called "the observing ego."
The ego has the capacity not only to be in the midst of life situa-
tions and react to them, and not only be filled with now this and
now that fantasy or urge, but also with the capacity to *observe
itself.* When we develop a capacity for a more or less constant
awareness of what is going on within us, then we acquire the
"observing ego," that is, an ego position which notes, observes,
and discriminates what is transpiring within consciousness at
any given time. This gives the ego a vantage point from which it
can say, "This is what is happening now . . . this is what I am feeling . . . this is the urge or fantasy at work in me." The development of these powers of self-observation greatly strengthens the
ego against the otherwise blind compulsions thrust upon it from
certain dangerous archetypes, and the fantasies and effects

which they engender. Both a relevant spiritual life and an effective psychotherapy will support the development of such an "observing ego."

Our defense against the power of evil, therefore, would seem to depend on three things: first, on our state of moral and psychological awareness; second, on some sense of moral and spiritual values; and third, on the quality of our relationships with other human beings. If these three things have been nourished in us and are given our due regard, then we have a certain freedom to choose the good and just over and against the evil and the unjust, but without them the power of evil is just too strong for an ego all too easily overcome by hubris and *atē*.

The matter of the strength of evil could not have been put more clearly than the way C. G. Jung phrased it in a letter to William W., one of the founders of Alcoholics Anonymous. Jung wrote:

> I am strongly convinced that the evil principle prevailing in this world leads the unrecognized spiritual need into perdition, if it is not counteracted by either a real religious insight or by the protective wall of human community. An ordinary man, not protected by an action from above and isolated in society, cannot resist the power of evil. (1953b, 624)

The Greeks and Jung and many others agree on the pervasiveness of evil in this sorry world in which we live. Jung suggests that a real religious insight is a protection against possession by evil. The Greeks would agree with Jung. They would say that the ultimate fault lies not in the gods but in ourselves, because through our own folly and the darkening of insight that comes from it, we bring upon ourselves sorrows and calamities which could have been avoided. So Homer has Zeus say to his assembled court, regarding the complaints of mortals:

> Look you now, how ready mortals are to blame the gods. It is from us, they say, that evils come, but they even of themselves, through their own blind folly (*atē*) have sorrows beyond that which is ordained. (1984, 1.32ff)

Note the words of Zeus, "beyond that which is ordained." It would seem that some calamities can be avoided by human beings if they would only resist the power of *atē*; however, certain other calamities are unavoidable. The Greek word involved here is the word *moira*. There are calamities that befall us because of *atē* and there are calamities that befall us because of *moira*. What is this *moira* which ordains for us a lot in life which cannot be avoided? To this we now turn; when we do, we find that we are in the midst of the most fundamental and important concept among the Greeks: the idea of fate.

Notes

1. The home of the Nez Percé Indians is in eastern Washington and northwestern Idaho. The name "Nez Percé" means "pierced nose" and is the white man's name for these interesting people. Their own name for themselves is Nimipu, which means roughly "the Real People." The Nez Percé story of Cannibal can be found in Aoki (1979). However, the motifs of this interesting story are worldwide, found not only in numerous other Native American stories, but also among peoples in India, Africa, and Tahiti, and among the Maori and Koryak.

2. Henceforth, the word *atē* refers to the psychological state of folly and sin which leads to ruin, and Atē (with the capital letter) refers specifically to the goddess who instills this condition in us.

3. It is interesting to compare the Greek story of Atē with the Christian story of Lucifer (Satan). Lucifer also once lived in heaven with God, but because of his malignity was cast out and "fell like lightning" to the earth. There is also a parallel in Jewish Scripture (the Old Testament) in the figure of Dame Folly, who entices all who pass her by to lives of wantonness and sin. See Proverbs 9:13–18.

4. Euripides *Hippolytus* 239ff. The last line means that a person who is made mad in love by *atē* at least does not realize at the time that he or she is being ruined.

5. For an analysis of the many Greek words for sin, as exemplified in the New Testament, see Sanford 1992. Cf. Dodds 1957, ch. 1.

6. This word is the most frequent Greek word used in the New Testament for conscience. It always connotes the ideas of both moral discrimination and consciousness. It occurs in Acts 23:1, 24:16; Rom. 2:15, 9:1, 13:5; 1 Cor. 8:7, 10, 12, 25; 2 Cor. 1:12, 4:2, 5:11; Tit. 1:15; Heb. 9:14; Jn. 8:9.

5

$\mathscr{F}$ATE AND $\mathscr{D}$ESTINY

$\mathscr{T}$oday, most of us believe that we are free to choose and shape our lives as we will. If something unpleasant happens to us, we may even be told by someone speaking in a very sincere voice, "Well, you know, you *chose* it." The fact is, however, that we were born into and live with a set of facts and circumstances quite beyond our control. The kind of parents we had are an example. Were our parents loving and helpful, or were they harsh and uncaring? The color of our skin is another factor over which we have no control. Were we born White? Brown? Black? The answer to this question is important because the color of our skin makes a difference in how our lives are going to be lived; it is part of our reality, a reality we can never change.

Where we were born also makes a difference. Were you born in basically affluent America, where the supermarkets are filled with food? Or were you born in Somalia or India, where many children grow up with emaciated bodies and sometimes stunted minds because they lacked even the basic nutrition that a growing child needs?

Countless other factors which we cannot change and which determine our lives are given to us in life. Were you born with a good mind or a dull one? With a strong, athletic body or a weak one? Did you receive a genetic inheritance which favors a healthy and successful life, or were you born with congenital diabetes or with genes that in midlife will afflict you with the terrible burden of Huntington's disease?

Then there are the outer circumstances of our lives. If you

were born male, when you became mature, did you find yourself drafted into the army and sent to fight a war? If you were in combat, were you wounded? Or did you escape unscathed while your buddy next to you was killed? If you married, did you and your marriage partner want and have children, or were you not blessed with a child, because of some malicious trick of nature? If you did have a child, was the child born healthy or impaired? Then there are the seemingly chance events which influence our lives so profoundly—fateful events which change our lives forever. Perhaps you were involved in an automobile accident for which you were not at fault. Was it really an "accident" that you were in the wrong place at the wrong time, or was there something inevitable about it? And finally, what of death, that fixed reality which awaits every one of us born into this world?

In everyone's life there are sets of circumstances like these which could not have been avoided, circumstances which constitute the "givenness" of our lives. For the ancient Greeks, the fact that our lives are shaped by fixed and unavoidable facts and circumstances was regarded as being of great importance; the Greeks saw their lives shaped by *moira*, a word which means a lot, share, or portion, and best rendered in English by our word *fate*. Ancient Greeks imagined that three goddesses allotted to each soul at his or her conception those fixed, unalterable events and circumstances which would influence that person's life for better or for worse, and would ultimately lead to that individual's final *moira*: his or her predetermined time of death. These goddesses were the three Moirae, or Fates. All of a person's life was lived within and shaped by the Fates. So powerful and influential were these triune goddesses that it is not too much to say that these deities—not the gods on Mt. Olympus—really presided over and determined human life.

A helpful image of how fate works is how the cards are dealt in a game of bridge or some similar card game. There are four players in the game of bridge, and they all play with the same fifty-two-card deck but, when the cards are dealt, each player receives a different hand. That hand may be good or bad, but the player cannot change it; the cards have been dealt, and each player in the game must play with what has been dealt to him or her. Fate works something like this. According to the ancient Greek view, we all live under the baleful influence of three goddesses of Fate, from whom each person receives his or her individual portion or share ("hand of cards"). Whatever that portion or share may be, that is the hand in life with which we must play the game.

Each of the three Moirae had a different function. Clotho, whose name means "the Spinster," spun the thread of life for each soul born into the world. Atropos, whose name means "the unchangeable, the inflexible, the unbending," cut the thread of a person's life at the preordained moment of that person's death. The third goddess, Lachesis, the "disposer of lots," apportioned to each soul those inescapable, fateful events and circumstances which would permanently shape that person's course of life in this world.

The Greeks had a number of stories about the inexorable nature of fate, and how, despite the best efforts of human beings to change or escape their fate, in the end it could not be done. One such story is the story of Meleager, the son of King Oeneus of Calydon and his wife, Althaea. At the time of the boy's birth, the Fates appeared to his mother and declared that he would live only so long as a brand then burning in the fire was not consumed. Althaea at once snatched the brand from the fire and put it in a safe place so it could not be burned. Some years later, however, after Meleager had grown to manhood, his father Oeneus forgot to sacrifice to Artemis. The enraged goddess took revenge by stirring up strife in the family, a quarrel that resulted in the murder of Althaea's brothers by her son, Meleager. When Althaea learned of this, she took the hidden brand and threw it in the fire, and as soon as it was consumed in the flames, Meleager died even as the Fates had decreed.

So powerful were the Fates that it was said they even assigned to the gods their places in the divine order. Even those deities of divine vengeance, the Erinyes, whom we will consider more deeply in the next chapter, once said that their divine task in life was given to them by the Fates. "For this is our office," they declared:

> . . . that ever-determining Fate, when it spun the thread of
> our lives, assigned unto us to hold unalterably: that upon
> those mortals on whom have come wanton murdering of

> kinsfolk, upon them we should attend until such time as
> they pass beneath the earth; and after death they [still] have
> no large liberty. (Aeschylus 1983b, 334–40, 389–95)

For the Fates and their awesome power were "honored everywhere among the gods" (Aeschylus 1983b, 967).

The truth of the matter is that as far as the lives of human
beings were concerned, the power and influence of the Moirae
was far greater and more important than that of Zeus. To be
sure, Zeus reigned supreme on Mt. Olympus, and he and the
other Olympian deities got all the headlines, but for the most
part he left the lives and affairs of human beings alone. The
deities who really ran the show, as far as what happened to mortals was concerned, were not the Olympians but the ancient
matriarchal deities: the Moirae, or Fates.

Indeed, when the Moirae had determined the fate of a mortal, it could not be changed even by the father of the gods, Zeus
himself. This Zeus found out when he had three sons born to
him from a mortal woman. Zeus wanted these three sons—Aea-
cus, Minos, and Rhadamanthus—to be free from the burden of
old age, but the Fates were relentless: the three were mortals,
said the Moirae, so they must endure the fate of old age; it was
their fate, and not even the will of Zeus could change it.

Fate could befall a deity as well as a mortal. Prometheus
was one of the Titans, old divinities who antedated the
Olympians, and he was also a benefactor of the human race. It
was Prometheus who saw that the first human beings were
weak, defenseless, naked creatures and was so moved with
compassion for them that he wanted to give them a gift to help
them with their lives—a gift of strength, or the power of flight,
or some other way of protecting themselves and making their
way in the world such as the various animals had been given.
But, alas! all the gifts had been given—save only the gift of fire—
and fire had been reserved as belonging to the gods alone.
Prometheus, however, was so deeply moved by the plight of
human beings that he stole some fire from heaven and gave it to
them; and with the help of fire, human beings were able to survive and make their way in the world. This act of kindness
brought down the wrath of Zeus upon Prometheus. As punishment for daring to steal fire from heaven, Zeus chained

Prometheus to a rock where he suffered eternal torment, some said from an eagle which Zeus sent each day to devour the liver of Prometheus, which would then grow back in the night only to be devoured again the next day. In this way, Prometheus suffered constant torture.

In Aeschylus's play *Prometheus Bound*, the Chorus urges Prometheus to refrain from benefitting mortals so he might yet be released from his bondage and torture. But Prometheus refuses, saying, "Nor thus, nor yet, is fulfilling Fate destined to bring this end to pass. When I have been bent by pangs and tortures infinite, thus only am I to escape my bondage. Art is feebler by far than Necessity." The Chorus then asks, "Who then is the steersman of Necessity?" (That is, where does the guiding power of necessity come from?) Prometheus replies that the power comes from "the triform Fates and the mindful Furies [Erinyes]." Incredulous that nothing can be done to change the fate of Prometheus, the Chorus asks, "Can it be that Zeus hath lesser power than they?" To which Prometheus replies, "*Aye, not even he can escape what is foredoomed*" (Aeschylus 1988, 511–4; emphasis mine).

Another example of the power of the Fates, which prevails even over the authority of Zeus, is found in that part of the *Odyssey* at which Odysseus presents himself to the court of King Alcinous because he wants protection; Odysseus knows that the king, being a god-fearing man, will heed the will of Zeus, who offers divine protection to all those who are worthy, who in their need come to those in power for help. So Alcinous gives Odysseus protection, and none can touch him; but Alcinous notes that when Odysseus finally leaves his land, which in time he must do, then "he shall suffer whatever Fate and the Dread Spinners [that is, Clotho, Atropos, and Lachesis] spun for him with their thread at his birth, when his mother bore him" (Homer 1984, 7.145–206).

Of special interest to psychology is a reference in Aeschylus's play, *The Eumenides*, which connects the dream to fate. The words are spoken by the ghost of Clytemnestra, who has appeared to her son Orestes—her murderer—in a dream. In Orestes' dream, Clytemnestra's ghost invokes the divine powers to avenge her murder. In her bitter diatribe about the cruelty of her death, Clytemnestra makes this statement: "For the mind

73

asleep hath clear vision, but in the daytime the fate of mortal man cannot be foreseen" (Aeschylus 1983b, 104–5). This saying connects fate with the message of our dreams. While we are awake, we do not see clearly what our fate is, but in our dreams our fate is clearly unfolded before our eyes. To put the matter in the language of our psychology: while the conscious mind goes along with the belief that it is seeing things clearly, there is actually a psychological process going on within us which determines our fate, that is, which way our lives and consciousness are going. The difference between our modern psychological attitude and that of the Greeks is that we believe that if we become aware of the message of our dreams, then what would have been the working out of inexorable fate can be changed, and a new direction can take place in our consciousness and in our lives. And who is this "I" who in sleep perceives the dream, this "dream ego" who is somehow akin to the waking ego but also different? It is none other than the soul itself, for in the dream, ego and soul are not separated as they are in waking life, and the dream ego, therefore, has the "eyes of the soul" with which to see the dream.

In addition to *moira*, the fixed fate allotted by the goddesses of fate, there was also *úpermoira*, a "fate over and beyond fate." *Úpermoira* was not a fate allotted at the time of the conception of the soul, nor was it a fate which could not have been avoided. It was, instead, a fate which individuals drew upon themselves, usually by acts of hubris and *atē* such as were described in chapter 4. The nature of *úpermoira* is that it could have been avoided because it was not decreed by the Fates themselves, but was the consequence of sin. Nevertheless, once such a fate had developed, it became as fixed and certain as *moira* itself. In our language we would say of those who suffered such a fate that "they brought it upon themselves."

In our culture the idea of a fixed fate no longer exists; what was for the Greeks the most powerful reality in human life has all but vanished from modern consciousness. This is partly because we no longer believe in the irrational forces of life, and partly because the Greek attitude has been largely eclipsed by the thinking of Christianity, Judaism, and Eastern philosophies and religious traditions. These religions have little room in them for fate.

In Hinduism and Buddhism, for instance, the idea of fate has given way to the ideas of *karma* and reincarnation. According to this view, the circumstances into which a soul is born into this world are not the capricious work of certain goddesses of fate, but reflect the moral and spiritual consequences of the soul's conduct in previous lives. If in your previous life you did evil deeds and remained spiritually ignorant, then in your next incarnation you might be born maimed from birth, or as a member of a lower caste, or at some point in your life meet with unfavorable events or circumstances. While the idea of fate as such finds no place in this Eastern way of looking at things, there is a resemblance between the Greek idea of *úpermoira* and the Eastern idea of *karma*, insofar as both ideas might say, of a person whose lack of awareness and perhaps selfish attitudes resulted in a disagreeable state of affairs, that "he brought it upon himself."

In post-biblical Christian thought, the idea of fate has been disregarded or outright rejected, as it was by Origen, Tertullian, Clement of Alexandria, Augustine, and other early Christian philosophers. The usual basis for the Christian rejection of fate was that it nullified the idea of free will. So the third-century Christian bishop Methodius argued:

> For, if we must speak plainly, he who lives according to the nature which belongs to him [i.e., Fate] in no way sins. For he did not make himself thus but Fate; and he lives according to its motion, being urged on by inevitable necessity.[1]

Of course, later in Christian thought the idea of Divine Providence develops, which determines the course and events of a person's life; but this is not fate. Divine Providence is purposive and part of the plan God has provided for a person's life, while fate partakes of the irrational: it just *is* and there is no "plan" to it.

Today we seldom think of ourselves and the circumstances of our lives as the result of capricious fate, much less as the result of a kind of divine dealing out of the cards. We may fancy ourselves above such notions, but the consequence is that we are often left in difficulty, in finding the proper spiritual and psychological attitude toward certain adverse life circumstances

75

that we cannot avoid. Without some way to find the proper attitude toward the irrational in life (fate), we will have difficulty in integrating our life experiences. To a large extent, whether or not that process of becoming whole which Jung called "individuation" will unfold in our lives depends on how we meet and live through the fated circumstances of our lives.

The Greeks left us a good story about the difference that it makes how a person goes to meet those fated circumstances of our lives which can be so frightening, especially how we go to meet our ultimate fate: death. In Sophocles' play *Antigone,* a soldier must take an unwelcome message to King Creon. As the messenger of bad news, he is justifiably afraid that he will be killed by the irate king, even though he is not responsible for what has happened. The soldier is so disheartened that he is well-nigh undone by his misery and fear. At last, however, driven by the necessity of finding a better attitude, Sophocles' character says,

> For plucking courage from despair methought
> "Let the worst hap," thou canst but meet thy fate. (1962, 235–6)

Armed with this attitude, the soldier goes to bring the king the unwanted message with his head held high.

From our contemporary point of view, we might frame our query as follows: If we are going to die, and if there is no life after death except as a "shade" in the land of Hades, god of the dead, as the Greeks for the most part believed, then what difference does it make whether we go to meet our death cringing with fear or with noble courage? Or, in other words, "if there is nothing in it for me, then what difference does it make?" The Greeks would have been shocked at such a nakedly egocentric attitude. For them, the noble course of action should always be pursued for its own sake—regardless of whether it would be rewarded or not. This is what makes action noble.

It is a psychological and spiritual fact, however, that if we must meet up with some dark and fated circumstances in our lives, then it does make a spiritual and psychological difference how we go to meet it. If, like the soldier in Sophocles' play, we go to meet what must be with courage, then we will be strengthened from within; in traditional language we would say that

God will be with us. Indeed, there are remarkable stories of people who have met the dark circumstances of their lives in just this way, and in so doing have found incredible strength.[2]

The same attitude Sophocles expressed in his play is also expressed in that Chinese book of wisdom, the *I Ching*. Consider the commentary by Richard Wilhelm on Hexagram 5: HSU (Nourishment). The Chinese text describes the proper attitude we must acquire when faced by difficulties and dangers which are fated and so cannot be avoided. Wilhelm writes:

> One is faced with a danger that has to be overcome. Weakness and impatience can do nothing. Only a strong man can stand up to his fate, for his inner security enables him to endure to the end. This strength shows itself in uncompromising truthfulness [with himself]. It is only when we have the courage to face things exactly as they are, without any sort of self-deception or illusion, that a light will develop out of events by which the path to success may be recognized. This recognition must be followed by resolute and persevering action. For only the man who goes to meet his fate resolutely is equipped to deal with it adequately. Then he will be able to cross the great water—that is to say, he will be capable of making the necessary decision and thus surmounting the danger. (1950, 25)

Although Christian theology, as we have noted, generally disregards or rejects outright the idea of fate, there are nonetheless a surprising number of passages in the New Testament which imply a belief in events or circumstances in life which *must be*, and so are akin to fate. The principal example would be the Cross of Christ. Because of its inevitability, the Cross looms as a fateful event, fixed by divine decree, an event which Jesus would have liked to avoid but knows that he must not and cannot do. So, Christ went to meet the fated event of the crucifixion with the correct attitude, and what was fate became destiny.

There is also, however, the cross that the followers of Christ must carry, for six times we read in the Gospels that those who are followers of Christ must take up their cross and follow him. So Jesus says in the Gospel of Matthew 10:38, "He who does not take up his own cross and follow me is not worthy of me." And in Luke's Gospel (9:23), we read: "If anyone will come after me let him deny himself and take up his cross daily."[3]

Whatever else the Cross of Christ represents, it is also symbolic of the work of individuation, symbolizing the necessity of carrying our own psychological and spiritual burden. The psychological aspect of this process is to recognize our own psyches and carry our psyches consciously. The unconscious way of going through life is to fail to recognize the various aspects of our larger Self and project the disagreeable ones, such as the shadow, onto others. When this happens, not only do we fail to know who we really are, but others are forced to carry our darkness for us. When this happens, then our individuation cannot take place; in religious language we would say then the purposes of God are thwarted. Spiritually, carrying the cross means to face resolutely whatever in life must be faced, be it within or from without, and to assume the burden of our personality— shadow, and all. The Cross thus represents our inescapable psychological and spiritual burden. It is our *moira*, and our fulfillment is not possible if we try to avoid it.

A second biblical allusion to fate is found in the ninth chapter of the Gospel According to John.[4] Jesus and his disciples are passing by when they see a man who was born blind. The disciples ask him: "Rabbi, who sinned, this man or his parents, that he was born blind?" Obviously something must lie behind this question, or else it would not have arisen in the minds of the disciples. The reason for the question is the idea which we find exemplified in the Old Testament (Jewish Scripture) that if someone is suffering, they must have done something to deserve it. God was the author of everything that took place in the world; evil events could not be laid at the foot of the devil because there was virtually no idea of the devil in the Old Testament. Indeed, there are only four references to Satan in the Jewish Scripture. Jewish Scripture evidences what could be called an "unflinching monotheism": whatever happened, be it desirable or undesirable, good or evil, illness or health, it came from God—for there was no other god but Jahweh. But God was also just, and being just, would not inflict evil, suffering, or disease on a person who did not deserve it for some moral infraction of God's will or divine law; therefore, if someone was ill, that person must have sinned.

That is why in the Book of Job, when Job is inflicted with boils and other misfortunes, his three "friends" insist that he must have sinned and should repent. Now, if a person had reached a mature age and then fallen ill, that person might well have committed a sin or sins of some sort, sufficient to justify God's afflicting him with or permitting him to suffer the disease. But what of a young child? Could it be said that a young child sinned? Or what of a baby, who like the blind man, was born into the world with an illness or affliction? In what sense could it be said that such a baby had sinned and so had merited misfortune?

If the setting of this story had been in India, it would have been said that the man was born blind because of a sin in a previous life, because of the widespread Indian belief in reincarnation. However, the idea of reincarnation never crossed the minds of the people of the Old Testament era; this is why they do not resort to this explanation as the reason for the man being born blind. But there was another possible explanation: perhaps the child had been born blind because of some sin of his parents. There was, in fact, a time in the era of the Old Testament when a belief existed that the sins of the fathers were visited upon succeeding generations. This idea, however, had been explicitly rejected by the later prophets, who firmly declared that each person was responsible only for his or her own sin. Jesus himself firmly rejected the idea that children bore the burden of their parents' sins when he answered the disciples' question by saying, "It was not that this man sinned, or his parents"; then he adds, "but that the works of God might be made manifest in him."[5]

Returning to the narrative in the Gospel of John, if this man's blindness was not because he had sinned, nor because his parents had sinned, nor due to a sin in a previous existence, then what was its origin? Jesus said that he was born blind so that the glory of God might be revealed in him. It could be said that it was this man's *fate* to be born blind; a disagreeable fate which the man did not deserve but, as is always the case with fate, could not be avoided. Hidden within this fate, however, was also his spiritual destiny, for as a result of his blindness he was later healed by Jesus, which not only brought him physical sight but also brought him spiritual sight, as is made clear later in the story. Thus, God's glory was not only manifested in the healing of the man's blindness, but also in the fulfillment of the purpose for which he was created.

A third example of the idea of fate in the New Testament is found in Paul's letter to the Galatians. In Galatians 6:2, Paul says to the Galatians, "Bear one another's burdens, and so fulfill the Law of Christ." But three verses later, in 6:5, Paul says, "For each man will have to bear his own burden." We seem to have a contradiction. First Paul says we should help others carry their burdens; three verses later he says that everyone will have to carry his or her own burden without help from anyone else.

The explanation for this seeming contradiction lies in the meaning of the two different Greek words Paul uses, one in 6:2 and the other in 6:5. In Galatians 6:2, Paul used the word *baros*, which means a "weight" or "pressure." It is the source of the word *barometer*, a device which measures the pressure or weight of air. In Galatians 6:5, though, Paul uses a different Greek word, *phortion*. The difference is that *baros* refers to a weight which anyone can carry, but *phortion* refers to a weight or burden which individuals must carry for themselves. For instance, in Greek the word *phortion* is the word used for a soldier's pack, the cargo of a ship, and the burden carried by a pregnant woman. Clearly a soldier must carry his own pack, as every man who has been in the army or marines knows very well. Similarly, once the cargo has been loaded into the hold of a ship and the ship has set out to sea, it will carry its load until it reaches its final destination. As for the load carried by a pregnant woman, not even the most feminist-minded husband can carry that for his wife; the burden is hers alone.

As we have noted, the biblical story of the man born blind suggests an enigmatic relationship between fate and destiny. We might approach this enigma by asking, "What is the relationship between fate and the process of individuation?" At first glance we might suppose that there is no relationship between these ideas because the word *fate* is not part of the Jungian vocabulary; indeed, there are only a few places in the voluminous collected works of C. G. Jung where the word *fate* is mentioned at all, and these passages are not of particular importance. Anima and animus, self, individuation, shadow, archetype—these are the "official" words which denote the basic ideas of Jungian psychology, but the word *fate* is not one of them. This is not surprising, since Jungian psychology tries to be intellectually and scientifically respectable, while the idea of fate partakes of the irrational and unscientific. Nonetheless, the idea of fate refuses to disappear. The fact is that there are certain realities in life which only the ancient vocabulary can adequately express. Words such as *fate, soul,* and *spirit* are among them. To be sure, we try our best to do without them; look up those three words, for instance, in a contemporary dictionary of psychology, and you will not find them listed. Apparently, psychology no longer regards itself as concerned with the soul; on the other hand, a psychology without the idea of a soul is "soul-less," and we all know instinctively what it means to say that someone or something is "without soul."

Fate, like soul, is one of those neglected but irreplaceable words we can't quite do without, and so it is not surprising to find that the Jungian writer, psychologist, and philosopher Edward Edinger has an interesting discussion of fate in his book, *Anatomy of the Psyche* (1985). Dr. Edinger suggests that fate is part of the alchemical symbolism of the *coagulatio*. The *coagulatio* is that stage in the alchemical process of transformation in which the elements in the alchemical retort become firm and solid. This refers to that stage in the process of individuation when we become firm and solid as personalities, that state in which, as a result of our inner process, a definite personality emerges. This process is assisted by fate which, as we have seen, acts like a necessity, binding us to certain inner and outer realities which we cannot escape. Only with the help of such necessities in our lives, Edinger points out, can our personalities become firm and our individuation become a fixed reality.

We might say that the *coagulatio*, which is made possible by enduring our fate, makes the difference between merely talking about individuation and actually undergoing it. There may well be a close and necessary relationship between everything in our life that is fated and the emerging in us of a completed personality. Looked at in this way, death itself, which is our ultimate fate, in this life at least, may not simply be a malignant and life-nullifying event but also the door through which we find our ultimate completion.

Whether or not we will find our ultimate completion,

however, will not simply be a matter of having a fate, but of how we go to meet that fate. This we discovered in contemplating the story of the frightened Greek soldier whose fate it was to bring bad news to the king, but found courage—and therefore his deepest self—in the thought that nothing more could happen to him than to meet his fate. The opposite of this would be a person who must now meet his or her fate, but who succumbs to cowardice or fear and cringes before it; this person is weakened, and perhaps the soul is even destroyed, by the fate that cannot be avoided.

Despite Jung having mentioned fate only a few times in his writings, and then mostly in passing, at least once he did suggest that our individuation is fulfilled by how we go to meet our fate. In this passage Jung speaks of a woman who was drawn by life into a frightening but fateful love relationship. Jung observed that if we must take the plunge into a dark encounter with a fateful event, we will need something like an attitude of trust in God and a willingness to persevere. Then he adds, "Thus, unsought and unexpected, the question comes in of one's religious attitude toward fate" (1953a, 7.164).

To meet our fate with courage requires from us, and develops within us, something called "character." Character is not a word we use very much today except perhaps to say, a bit pejoratively, "So-and-so is quite a character." As writer Charles Upton has pointed out, character is neglected in our culture in favor of "personality."[6] The word *character* comes from a Greek word *xaractēr*, which means a stamp or imprint. Thus, to have "character" is to be someone definite, defined. Personality, on the other hand, suggests a kind of showiness, a mode of displaying oneself, an image of ourselves we project out for others to see. Psychologically, it is closely related to the word *persona*. Upton argues that we have become such a personality culture that many of our recent presidents were elected not on the basis of their character but because of their personality. Personality is showy and exciting and gets the center of the stage; it appeals to a culture like ours which is addicted to excitement and so requires injections of excitement from its entertainers and, perhaps, also from its leaders. In contrast, character tends to be steady, quiet, understated, and in the background—but it is character which pulls a person through when the chips are down.

Character, Upton says, is created in us by living according to certain principles, principles to which a person remains true even though it brings him or her into an unpleasant confrontation with others who are less high-minded. By adhering to principles, even when it is difficult or disadvantageous to do so, we develop strength of character. This strength of character is not necessarily sought directly, but when it is found, it is desired for its own sake, not for any rewards. It can be said that when a person goes to meet his or her fate—with courage if it be a dark fate, or with gratitude and modesty if it be a favorable one—then that person further develops that depth, strength, and firmness we call character.

When we go to meet our fate in this way, we are also accompanied by what could be called "the grace of God." The idea of the grace of God is not from Greek mythology as such, but the word *grace* does come from a Greek word: *charis*, a word we have already noted which means a freely given gift of God. This grace, or *charis*, comes to those who have resolutely determined to follow their appointed path in life no matter where it may lead them. Through developing character, and the help of the *charis* of God, we find our perfection.

Perfection. The idea of perfection has become virtually a bad word in some psychological circles, because it has been associated with "trying to be perfect"—that is, without any blemishes, darkness, or shadow. As Jungian psychology helps us understand, trying to be perfect in this latter sense of the word develops a faulty character, because while there is an outward display of goodness or purity, inwardly there is the unrecognized darkness. Thus, most people who strive for what is commonly recognized as perfection develop a persona of goodness which is contradicted by the shadow within. Because such people lack contact with their shadow, they also, for all their vaunted "perfection," lack depth and, quite often, human warmth.

But there is another sense of the word *perfection* which is psychologically and spiritually relevant. We can say that something is "perfect" when it has become the utmost possible expression of what it is meant to be. Let us imagine an automobile mechanic who has been working on a V-8 engine. First he studies the engine. Then he replaces any faulty parts. Then he adjusts all the parts so that they function together in exactly the right way, and finally he does the "fine tuning." When at last he believes everything is operating in the engine just as it should, he then turns on the engine and *listens* to it. He listens because a good mechanic can tell how well an engine is running by the sound it makes. If the mechanic is able to hear that quasi-melodious and harmonious sound a V-8 engine makes when all of its many parts are operating correctly, synchronously, and smoothly, then he may well say to himself with satisfaction, "Perfect!"

Psychologically and spiritually, something like this may also develop with us. As we understand, develop, and use all of the various parts of our personality, including the recognition of the shadow of which we have just spoken, then we begin to become whole; but we are not perfected until life has tried us in such a way that the very best has been brought out in us.

Quite often this perfection of the self will be brought out only through some particular life experience or circumstance; analysis alone cannot accomplish the task. A Jewish client of mine related the following story (which I tell with his permission) to explain how it happened that the only family he knew when he was a child was his mother and father and one aunt with her only child. When I asked why he had no extended family other than this, he explained that they all—except for his parents, and for this aunt and her son—had been killed in the Holocaust. When I inquired why the aunt and her son had survived when the others did not, he told me the following story. In the middle of World War II, his aunt, at the time a young woman, and her infant son were being led with other people to be executed by a firing squad. The place of the execution was on the Russian-Polish border, and the time was late in the day; indeed, it was already becoming dark. When the young mother, clasping her infant to her breast, was marched past the German soldier assigned to shoot her, the soldier whispered to her, "When I shoot, run!" Then, when the commanding officer gave the order to shoot, the soldier shot into the air; the young woman ran with her child into the darkness, somehow managing to escape, and lived to tell the story.

We could say that it was the German soldier's fate to be the man assigned to shoot the young mother and her child, but when he chose not to shoot to kill, but to fire harmlessly into the air, then the soldier met his destiny. Fate is inevitable; our destiny we may fulfill or fail to fulfill. Thus, whether or not we fulfill our destiny has a relationship with how we meet our fate, and with the fateful choices that we make at crucial moments in our lives.

We do not know what happened to the German soldier. Perhaps no one noticed, and he was able to continue being a soldier until he was either killed in the war or lived on after the war was over. More than likely it was noticed by the officers that he had failed to kill his intended victim and that he was himself executed. Whatever happened, it could be said that at the moment when the soldier chose not to shoot, he reached a certain perfection as a human being because he then *expressed the finest in himself*. How did he find the courage not to shoot? Perhaps it was through the *charis*, the divine grace, which enabled him not to escape that fate which confronted him with his terrible choice, but to make a choice that led to his perfection as a human being.

Notes

1. Methodius 1957, ch. 16. Cf. Martyr 1957, 43; Augustine 1978, 5.1; Origen 1984, 3.5. Unfortunately, Tertullian's treatise on fate is lost.
2. In this way Admiral Stockdale was able to endure nine years of torture and solitary confinement in a North Vietnamese prison, and survive both physically and psychologically. See Sanford 1984, 328–32.
3. Matt. 10:38 and Luke 9:23, Revised Standard Version. Cf. Matt. 16:24; Mark 8:34 and 10:21; Luke 14:27.
4. For more discussion of this story, see Sanford 1993.
5. John 9:2. For a detailed discussion of this story, see Sanford 1992, 20–22.
6. Quotes and references to Upton's work are from his 1993 book, *Hammering Hot Iron: A Spiritual Critique of Bly's* Iron John.

6

AVENGING THE MOTHER

In our discussion of Atē, and also in our chapter on the Fates, we have already mentioned those deities of feminine vengeance called the Erinyes in Greek, or known in English translations as the Furies. We also met them briefly in our discussion of that deity of vengeance and retribution, Nemesis. The time has come to explore the nature of these goddesses in more depth.

By now it will not come as a surprise to the reader to learn that there were three Erinyes. The triune nature of the goddesses, as we have noted, apparently stems from the three phases of the moon; this marks the Erinyes as belonging to the old matriarchal deities, and distinguishes them from the more masculine Olympians. Their connection with the ancient order of goddesses is also clear from their birth; they were born to Gaia—from whose name we derive our word *geography*—the old Mother Goddess whose name means "earth," after she was made fruitful from the bloody drops which fell from the severed phallus of the sky god, Ouranos.

In keeping with their ancient origins, the Erinyes did not dwell on Mt. Olympus but were said to live in dreadful Tartarus, a part of the underworld reserved for those mortals who had committed some grievous offense against the gods. So, at least, said Apollo, who referred to the Erinyes as:

[L]oathsome maidens . . . with whom nor any god nor man nor beast consorteth ever. For evil's sake were they even born, since they inhabit the evil gloom of Tartarus beneath the earth—creatures loathed of men and of Olympian gods. (Aeschylus 1983b, 70–4)

The Furies carried torches, serpents, and whips; and perhaps in recognition of their violent nature, they were given in Athens a sanctuary beneath the hill of the war-loving god Ares. We are told by Aeschylus that the Erinyes flew but without need of wings, and that from their nostrils emanated fearsome blasts of repulsive air, while a noxious fluid oozed from their eyes (1983b, 52–4). When enraged, the Erinyes would leap down on men from their vantage point in the air like birds of prey, smashing them quickly with the heavy-falling force of their clawed feet (370–1). The Furies were so dreaded that it was believed to be dangerous to refer to them by their proper name "the Erinyes," lest they take offense at being called "the Furious Ones." Instead a euphemism was used and they were often referred to as the Eumenides, which means "the Blessed Ones"; this became the name of the play about them by Aeschylus which we will examine shortly. Their individual names are also suggestive of their functions in the divine economy of ancient Greece: Allekto, whose name derives from a Greek word *allektos*, which means "unceasing, implacable"; Tisiphone, whose name denotes "the relentless one"; and Megaira, whose name means "envious anger" and derives from a Greek word *megairo*, which means "to grudge a thing."

The Erinyes are on the side of what could be called the primal feminine values. One of these is faithfulness in love. To betray love can bring down the wrath of the one who has been betrayed upon the head of the betrayer. "Hell hath no fury like a woman scorned" is a quotation many a man—and some women too—have experienced first hand. This "hellish fury" was the theme of Euripides' play *Medea*. In this timeless Greek saga, Medea and her husband Jason have been exiled to the realm of King Creon, where Jason makes it a point to befriend the king and to charm the king's daughter, Princess Creusa. Medea, however, is left out of all this. Eventually it is decided by King Creon and Jason that Jason should marry the princess. Jason informs Medea of his plan, explaining carefully that all of this is for the sake of the welfare of Medea herself and for their two sons; they will all benefit, he says, because he will be able to provide for them and protect them after he has married into the royal family. Medea, though, is definitely not pleased. She vows vengeance and calls upon the bloodthirsty spirit that dwells in a woman who has been wronged in love:

> Woman quails at every peril,
> Faint-heart to face the fray and look on steel;
> But when in wedlock-rights she suffers wrong,
> No spirit more blood-thirsty shall be found.
> (Euripides 1979c, 1251–60)

Lacking any political power, Medea falls back on the only power she has: she will make Jason suffer for his unfaithfulness in love by killing their two children; she will revenge herself on Creon and Creusa by sending Creusa a gown so beautiful that no woman could resist putting it on, but first steeping the garment in poison, so that whoever comes into contact with it will receive the poison into their body and die an agonizing death. In time, all of this comes about. Medea slays the children to make their father suffer, and not only does Princess Creusa die when she dons the poisoned robe, but her father King Creon dies as well when he tries to save her by stripping the robe away.

Just prior to this act of terrible vengeance for a love that has been scorned, the Chorus makes a plea to Mother Earth (Gaia) that the tragedy be averted, calling upon Earth's daughters, the Erinyes, to restrain the hand of Medea:

> O Earth, O all-revealing splendour
>> Of the Sun, look down on a woman accurst,
>> Or ever she slake the murder-thirst
> Of a mother whose hands would smite the tender
>> Fruit of her womb.
> Look down, for she sprang of thy lineage golden:
> Man's vengeance threatens—thy seed are holden
>> 'Neath the shadow of doom!
> But thou, O heaven-begotten glory,
> Restrain her, refrain her: the wretched, the gory
> Erinyes by demons dogged, we implore thee,
>> Snatch thou from yon home!
> (Euripides 1979c, 1230ff)

The Erinyes, however, do not heed the prayer of the Chorus, from which we can conclude that they were so in sympathy with Medea's rage that they would not restrain her hand from the terrible deed she was contemplating. Though the text does not say it in so many words, we can suspect the Erinyes, the spirits of feminine vengeance, inspired Medea's plot.

Our best source of information about the Erinyes, however, is the aforementioned play by Aeschylus, *The Eumenides*, which is the third play in the trilogy known as the *Oresteia*, which also includes *Agamemnon* and *The Choephorae*, and which concerns the events that befall Agamemnon's family after his victorious return from Troy. Prior to the trilogy's action, Agamemnon, King of the Greeks, assembles a naval expedition to recover the beautiful Greek princess Helen from the Trojans, for the Greeks claimed that Helen had been abducted by the Trojan prince Paris. With the vessels ready and the soldiers gathered to enter the ships and sail across the sea to the land of the Trojans (what is now Turkey), Agamemnon's forces face a seemingly insurmountable delay: there is no wind. The goddess Artemis has stayed the winds from aiding the Greeks because Agamemnon has slain one of her sacred deer, and the goddess will relent only if King Agamemnon sacrifices his only daughter, Iphigenia. This Agamemnon eventually does, after great inner struggle and in opposition to the wishes of Clytemnestra—his wife and Iphigenia's mother. The sacrifice performed, Artemis allows favorable winds to send the Greek fleet and soldiers on to Troy. After many years of violent struggle the Trojans are defeated, and the weary Greeks are able to return home. In Agamemnon's absence, however, Clytemnestra has taken a second husband, Aegisthus. When Clytemnestra learns Agamemnon is returning, she and Aegisthus plot to murder him. This murder they commit, to the bitter grief and angry dismay of Orestes, the son of Clytemnestra and Agamemnon, and also to the dismay of the god Apollo, who orders Orestes to avenge his father's death. Orestes then returns from exile to murder both Aegisthus and his own mother, Clytemnestra.

At this point the Erinyes appear, filled with wrath at Orestes' matricide. It makes no difference to them that Orestes had a just cause in avenging his father's death; Orestes has committed the worst possible offense against the code which the

Erinyes defend: the rights and sanctity of family—and especially the mother. They declare:

> For this is the office that ever-determining Fate, when it
> span the thread of our life, assigned unto us to hold unal-
> terably: that upon those of mortals on whom have come
> wanton murdering of kinsfolk, upon them we should
> attend until such time as they pass beneath the earth; and
> after death they have no large liberty. (Aeschylus 1983b,
> 328–40)

The Furies then place this curse upon Orestes:

> O'er our victim consecrate, this is our song—fraught with
> madness, fraught with frenzy, crazing the brain, the Furies'
> hymn, spell to bind the soul, untuned to the lyre, withering
> the life of mortal man. (341–6)

Orestes tries desperately to escape the avenging Erinyes, but
they follow him relentlessly. Speaking with one voice, the mer-
ciless goddesses say:

> . . . In wingless flight I came in pursuit of him over the sea,
> swift as a swift ship. So now, somewhere hereabout he must
> be crouching. The smell of human blood makes me laugh
> for joy! (248–53)

When they finally find Orestes, the Erinyes cry out in fierce joy:

> Thou art bound in requital to suffer that I suck the ruddy
> clouts of gore from thy living limbs. May I feed myself on
> thee—a gruesome draught! (263–4)

One might suppose that mighty Zeus would interfere to curb
the powers of these dreadful female deities, whom he called
"creatures loathed of men and of the Olympian gods . . . a hate-
ful and blood-streaming band," but Zeus is so repelled by them
that he will have nothing to do with anyone who is assailed by
them (73–4; 365–6).

At the end of this gory tale, the goddess Athena succeeds
in arranging a compromise. A trial is held, and Athena is the
judge who hears both sides of the story: the angry pleas for

vengeance of the Erinyes, and Orestes' defense of his own act of vengeance. A jury who hears these arguments is divided in its final opinion, but Athena casts the tie-breaking vote and Orestes is acquitted. Needless to say, the Erinyes are indignant at this outcome, but perhaps having been partly placated by the dignity they were given in the trial, they allow themselves to be appeased with the offer of a permanent abode and place in the land.

An interesting aspect of this trial takes place when Apollo appears on behalf of his client, Orestes. Apollo argues that Clytemnestra had no right to dispute Agamemnon's decision to sacrifice Iphigenia in order to win the favor of Artemis because, as the mother, she was not really the parent at all; she only provided a womb in which the masculine seed could be nourished. The man is the real parent, Apollo says, not the mother:

> The mother of what is called her child is not its parent, but only the nurse of the newly implanted germ. The begetter [i.e., the man] is the parent, whereas she, as a stranger for a stranger, doth but preserve the sprout, except God shall blight its birth. (657–61)

Apollo then proceeds to give what he regards as a convincing proof by citing the case of Athena, who was born when she sprang from the head of her father Zeus without benefit of a mother:

> And I will offer thee a sure proof of what I say: fatherhood there may be, when mother there is none. Here at hand is a witness [Athena], the child of Olympian Zeus—and she not so much as nursed in the darkness of the womb, but such a scion as no goddess could bring forth. (662–66)

In both *Medea* and *The Eumenides*, we see feminine justice at work with a ruthless intensity. In both cases it is evoked by a sin against a primal love relationship: in *Medea*, the relationship of lovers violated by Jason's ambitions; and in *The Eumenides*, the relationship of the mother to the daughter violated by Agamemnon's sacrifice of Iphigenia so as to make possible the accomplishment of his masculine purpose of making war against the Trojans. Notice that in *The Eumenides*, the Erinyes did not persecute Clytemnestra for her murder of her husband. This is because the relationship of Clytemnestra and Agamemnon was not a blood relationship but a marital one, and because her murder atoned for Agamemnon's betrayal of the ancient matriarchal code of mother and child.

Wherever the laws of eros and of the natural order of things are violated, there we see emanating from life that dark energy of retribution exemplified in the Erinyes. We have already noted the statement, "Hell hath no fury like a woman scorned." But in men, as well as in women, anger can emerge from the feminine which has an Erinyes-like fury when the elemental values of relationship have been violated. This deep Erinyes anger can also emerge within the individual personality, when the realm of the unconscious psyche has been spurned. The unconscious can turn toward consciousness a dark and dreadful aspect. It can become destructive when it is neglected, and in its vindictiveness it can poison consciousness, or bring about calamities in our outer lives such as accidents. This is the reason Jung once said that the unconscious turns toward us a face which reflects our attitude toward it.

Earth itself can react darkly when its natural order has been wantonly violated. As we noted in our chapter on Themis, there is a "Right Order" in nature which we ignore or violate to our peril. The Erinyes, in their function as guardians of the world of the Mother, were represented in Greek mythology as capable of afflicting the land itself with pestilence in reaction to a wanton disregard by human beings of the rights of nature as our Mother. So Athena says of them:

> These women have an office that does not permit them lightly to be dismissed; and if they fail to gain the victory in their cause, the venom from their resentment will fall upon the ground and become hereafter an intolerable and perpetual pestilence to afflict the land. (476–9)

Conversely, when nature is honored by the observance of her requirements and laws, then these same powers bless the land.

This is another reason for the other name for the Erinyes, the Eumenides, which is not only a euphemism to avoid saying the name out loud of these dread powers, lest utterance of their very name bring them down upon the speaker. It is also an apt name to give to powerful feminine deities who can produce abundance and blessing as well as destruction and vengeance. In nature, everything is related to everything else. When this interlocking web of relationships prevails and is not disrupted, then nature preserves a creative balance that favors the abundance of life, but when she is disrupted or violated, then nature produces ruin. All this is "Erinyes," and that is the way it is, for the Greeks always tell things the way they really are.

The Erinyes, however, were not alone in their defense of the feminine and its prerogatives. Another deity joined them in this defense. A latecomer to the scene of Greek mythology, the man/woman god Dionysus has justly been called "the strangest god of them all." To him we now turn.

7

$\mathscr{D}$IONYSUS:

THE STRANGEST GOD
OF THEM ALL

$\mathscr{D}$ionysus stands apart from all the other Greek deities. He is not one of the Olympians, for he appeared on the Greek scene at a late date; neither is he one of the old goddesses like Ananke or the Moirae. The fact is that Dionysus is a reality unto himself, or perhaps we should say unto "herself," for nothing about Dionysus is firm and distinct, including the god's sexuality. Sometimes Dionysus appears masculine; at other times his feminine characteristics emerge so strongly that one wonders if the god is more man or woman.

In keeping with his complex nature, Dionysus was given many epithets. He was called *purigetes*, "the one born of fire," *sukites*, "the one of the fig tree," *polygethes*, "the one filled with joy," and *kissodomos*, "ivy-crowned." He was *dendritos*, "the tree god," *gunaimanes*, "the inspirer of frenzied women," and was also known as *phales*, "the friend of the phallus," for reasons we will explore later. In addition to these epithets, the god also had many names. In addition to his primary name Dionysus, the derivation of which is uncertain, he was also called Bromios, which means the sounding or boisterous, and was referred to by the mystic name of Iacchus. In his *Metamorphoses*, the Latin poet Ovid lists eight names for this many-faceted god.

Dionysus was a shape-shifter, a god who could appear in many theriomorphic guises. He was closely associated with the bull, perhaps because of the bull's phallic powers, and also with the serpent; sometimes serpents were said to be entwined in his hair. Hell-hounds often accompanied the god on his revelries, and he was frequently shown as a lion into whose likeness he could transform himself at will. He was especially associated with the goat, perhaps because of his capricious ways (the word "capricious" coming from the Latin word *caper*, goat); indeed, his devotees celebrated a kind of communion with the god in which they drank the blood of goats to imbibe the spirit of the god into themselves.

Dionysus is a god of paradox par excellence. He was the deity of wildness and abandonment and of the most blessed deliverance from the many constraints of life; however, he was not the god of lawlessness, for he had his own law to which people were called, however strange that law might appear from a conventional viewpoint. Had Dionysus been a god of lawlessness, he might have had as one of the epithets the Greek word *panourgos*, a word which means literally "anything goes" (and which appears in the New Testament as one of the words for lawless evil). This word was not associated with Dionysus, though; on the contrary, he taught mortals they should be obedient unto heaven, honor the gods, and walk in the ways of justice (Euripides 1979a, 991–1015). Likewise, while a fierce avenger to his enemies, he was not a deity of war but of peace (419). And though he was the god of wine and intoxicated delight, neither was he the god of wanton drunkenness, at least not until the Romans took him over, and he began to appear in degenerate forms and became known as Bacchus.

Far from being a wanton god, Dionysus was a god with a mission, a mission which he himself declared "to be god manifest to mortals" (Euripides 1979a, 22). The revelation of the divine to humankind was made known by Dionysus in a *mustērion*, a "mystery" in the ancient Greek sense of a secret knowledge which could only be known through undergoing an initiatory experience.[1] This *mustērion* of Dionysus was so deep and so uncanny that it amounted to an understanding of the mystery of life itself. Most of all, Dionysus was the god of *mania*, or "madness"—a madness so strange and wonderful that to understand it was to understand both the *mustērion* of the god and the meaning of life itself. Before we can presume to know more about this strange madness of Dionysus, however, we must know more about the god himself: his origins, his many stories, and the nature of his appeal to the ancient Greeks.

That Dionysus emerged into the life of Greece later than either the matriarchal deities we have been considering or the Olympians leads many scholars to believe that his origins were not in Greece but from some distant realm. There is, however, no agreement among them on the locale from which his cult emerged. Some say that he came originally from Phrygia (Asia Minor), where he was associated with the Asiatic mother goddess Cybele, a theory supported by an allusion to the mystery rites of Cybele in Euripides' play about Dionysus, *The Bacchanals*. Others, however, say that the cult of Dionysus came from Greece itself, albeit from some of its more remote regions. From the point of view of our psychology, the true origin of Dionysus lies in that archetypal layer of the human psyche from which emerges the creative imagination underlying all mythology. From this point of view, Dionysus portrays an integral part of our unconscious psychic life; he personifies and dramatizes an energy imbedded deeply within our human nature, perhaps in all of life. Thus, from the hidden places of the human heart the god calls for expression—and offers to mortals his own peculiar kind of freedom (Euripides 1979a, 72–88).

We may speculate that the cult of Dionysus burst upon the ancient world when it did in order to fill a psychological and spiritual need, perhaps to compensate for an emerging cultural tendency to identify too much with the rational at the expense of those life-giving energies of the irrational which alone can bring freedom to the soul. But before we can understand the nature of this Dionysian freedom that the god offers, we must first learn more about this most paradoxical of all the gods who was called "a god most terrible, yet kindest unto humankind"(Euripides 1979a, 861).

Dionysus was said to have been conceived in the womb of the mortal woman, Semele, who was the daughter of the Greek hero Cadmus, founder of the city of Thebes. The seed from which Dionysus sprang was not, however, from a mortal man but from Zeus. The story is that when Hera learned of the love affair between Zeus and Semele and of Semele's conception of a child by their union, Zeus's wife was so enraged that she conceived a plot to destroy the offending mother and her unborn child. This she sought to accomplish by persuading Semele to pray that Zeus would show himself to her in all of his divine glory. So Semele prayed, and Zeus reluctantly responded to her prayerful request. But, alas! the naked splendor of the god was so great that Semele was overwhelmed by the sight and destroyed by Zeus's lightning. When Zeus beheld the tragedy, he swooped down from heaven and tore the unborn child from Semele's womb; he then placed the child in his own thigh, from which in due course Dionysus was born, a god-man, conceived in the womb of a mortal, by the seed of a god, and born from the thigh of Zeus.

One would think that Hera would have been content with the punishment she had imposed on Semele, but according to another version of the story in which Semele does not die, Hera remained so consumed by jealousy that she drove Semele and her husband Athamas mad. The infant Dionysus was then entrusted by Zeus to the care of nymphs who dwelt on a mountain so remote that to this day its exact location is unknown. Here the nymphs nurtured the strange child on wild honey. This detail is symbolically meaningful, for honey is the product of bees, and of all forms of life, bees are seen as the most feminine and matriarchal, since all the male bees are killed at birth save for those few necessary to impregnate the queen bee. That Dionysus was nurtured on wild honey underscores the powerful influence of the feminine on him from his earliest days.

When Dionysus was grown to manhood, he began his wanderings. In one of the oldest stories about his adventures, the wandering Dionysus was seized by pirates and bound to the mast of their ship, but when the ship was far out at sea, the cords which bound the god fell away from him as though by magic, and a vine grew mysteriously about the ship's mast. Dionysus then changed himself into a lion, which so terrified the pirates that they leapt into the sea, where they were changed by the god into dolphins.

In these stories of the birth of Dionysus and the awesome way in which the god disposed of the pirates, we see both the favor that he was given by the women—as exemplified in the devotion to him of his mother Semele—and his awesome power to shift shapes, appearing now in this form and then in another to strike awe into his devotees and fear into the hearts of his enemies.

Another story which exemplifies the magical powers of the god and his love for women is found in the legend of Theseus and Ariadne. Theseus was the Greek hero who freed the people of Athens from the terrible tyranny imposed on them by Minos, King of Crete. It seems that Minos, whose power was greatly feared throughout the ancient world of Hellas, had imposed on the Greeks an annual tribute of seven youths and seven maidens, all in the fairest bloom of life. These young men and women were taken to the island of Crete and placed in a bewildering labyrinth inhabited by the monstrous bull-like Minotaur, who lived on human flesh. So intricate was the labyrinth in which the fearful beast dwelt that no one who entered it had ever found a way out. Trapped inside the serpentine maze of corridors, the youths and maidens would soon be destroyed by the Minotaur as he roamed through the labyrinth in search of prey.

However, one year, the hapless victims were saved by Theseus, who when the time came for the annual tribute to King Minos to be made, volunteered to go. As luck would have it, when the intended victims reached Crete, the princess of the land, Ariadne, beheld Theseus and fell in love with him. When the sacrificial victims, including Theseus, were led into the labyrinth, Ariadne (whose name is akin to the Greek word for spider—*araxne*) gave Theseus a marvelous thread. As the victims were led deeper and deeper into the labyrinth, Theseus, following Ariadne's instructions, trailed the thread behind him. When the Minotaur attacked the victims, the hero succeeded in destroying the monster; then, by means of the thread, he led the Greek youths and maidens out of the labyrinth and eventually to safety. Ariadne, filled with love for Theseus, gladly left her native land and fled with him to Greece. But, alas! Theseus faithlessly abandoned his benefactor, deserting her on a remote island. Here, exiled from her father's kingdom and abandoned by her beloved, Ariadne wept alone until she was discovered by Dionysus, who loved her, made her his bride, and took her away to safety.

The story of Dionysus's love for Ariadne typifies the god's

love for women generally, many of whom responded to his love by becoming devoted followers. These followers were known as maenads (*mainades*), a name which means "the mad women," not because they were insane but because they were filled with and inspired by the god. Dionysus was also closely associated with many feminine deities; with the Charitēs, for instance, whom we have already had occasion to discuss, with Aphrodite, and with the Muses, those feminine deities of music, song, dance, and the arts from whose name we derive such words as *music* and *museum*. Doubtless because of his affinity to the Muses, later in his career Dionysus became the patron deity of the theater; indeed, the memory of the god is still revered among many actors and musicians today.

Dionysus also was the god of the phallus, and in processions held periodically in his honor, his devotees carried images of the phallus. The association between Dionysus and the phallus has to do not only with his sexual prowess, but also with the god's connection with nature. Dionysus is a god of life-generating energy, and the phallus is that potent instrument which fertilizes the feminine and promotes life. It was said that wherever the god went, flowers bloomed and the world turned lush and green, for the ecstatic energy of the god is the energy of life itself. Here, too, we see another connection between Dionysus and Aphrodite, referred to elsewhere in classical texts as "member-loving Aphrodite."

Dionysus was also closely associated with that most *yin* of all elements: water. Greek scholar Water F. Otto writes:

> Water is the element in which Dionysus is at home. Like him it betrays a dual nature: a bright, joyous and vital side; and one that is dark, mysterious, dangerous, deathly . . . Dionysus comes out of the water and returns to it . . . he has his place of refuge and home in the watery depths. (Otto 1981)

Thus, Dionysus partakes of the nature of both wine and water; he brings the temporary dissolution of the ego in sleep, and through the wine he brings joy to the soul, but he also brings with him much that is dark, mysterious, and dangerous as well as life-giving.

Dionysus was kind and generous to those who were his

friends but ruthless and destructive to those who rejected him. As Plutarch tells us, when Minyas and his daughters rejected Dionysus and resisted his cult, the god drove them mad, and in their madness the frenzied women tore their own children to pieces. As though this was not sufficient punishment, Dionysus then turned these women who had despised him into bats. Why bats? Perhaps because the bat is a "crazy" creature—a flying mammal—and the women, having rejected the divine madness of the god, were punished by the craziness symbolized by the bat. Clearly, this god of ecstasy symbolizes a power which can work for either good or ill, which can either fill a soul with joy, peace, and oblivion to the pains and disappointments of life or send upon a person a dreadful fate.

One of the greatest of the gifts of Dionysus was the knowledge of the making of wine, for before Dionysus came to teach them, mortals did not know the secret by which the grape could be made to yield its healing and intoxicating nectar. It was said that the gift of wine was bestowed on mortals by the god because of the kindly reception given him by Icarius of Athens. In his wanderings about the earth Dionysus was often rejected, but Icarius received him hospitably, took him into his home, provided for him, and without thought of any reward treated him generously. In gratitude for his kindness, Dionysus gave Icarius the knowledge of wine-making, and this knowledge soon spread far and wide, and brought the cheer of wine to hearts weary with the griefs and struggles of life.

Dionysus did not give wine in the spirit of common drunkenness, however; that was the work of Bacchus, who as we have already noted, was a Romanized and degenerate version of Dionysus. Dionysus was not the god of the extinction of consciousness as we experience it in drunkenness, but the god of the release of spirit and the animation of the soul. Nonetheless, if the power of the god was imbibed recklessly, it could be dangerous, for which reason Dionysus was sometimes represented as accompanied by the Sileni, paradoxical beings who were both accomplished musicians and drunken satyrs. Dionysus's wine, however, did not usually bring drunken oblivion, but stilled the tears of humanity and brought joy, for Dionysus, though he himself often endured great sorrows, was the god of joy, a god who though he could be fiercely destructive to his enemies also had deep compassion for the suffering of mortals. So it was said of Dionysus that he was "the Lord [who] wept to still the tears of mortals . . . so the joy of men [and women] flows forth from the tears of a god."[2]

Equally important, this god of kindness also bestowed on weary mortals the gift of healing sleep, that sleep in which we find surcease from our pain and refreshment of the spirit, a sleep in which the weary ego can dissolve itself in the mysterious world of sleep and dreams and awake in the morning renewed—by the power of the god! So Euripides says of him:

> The [grape] cluster's flowing draught he found, and gave
>   to mortals,
> Which gives rest from grief to men
> Woe-worn, soon as the vine's stream filleth them.
> And sleep, the oblivion of our daily ills,
> He gives—there is none other balm for toils.
> He is the gods' libation, though a god,
> So that through him do humankind attain good things.
>   (Euripides 1979a, 279–85)

There were many other stories about the god, including one account in which he was said to have wandered throughout the world, even as far as India, and how he was initiated into the mysteries of Rhea, another version of the ancient Earth-mother goddess akin to Cybele. The most important story of all, however, is found in Euripides' play, *The Bacchanals*. If someone had to choose only one of the various stories about Dionysus to study, this play by Euripides would clearly stand out as the one to read. First, we will summarize the story which Euripides tells us; then, we will look at its meaning.

As the story begins Dionysus is traveling throughout the world to make himself known, and eventually his path leads him to Thebes. Here he is well received by two old men, Tiresias the blind seer, and Cadmus, who in his youth was a famous hero. However, when Pentheus, king of the land, hears of the arrival of Dionysus, he rejects him and his claim to be a god; he disdains Dionysus's feminine ways and plans to imprison him. Further, Pentheus is scornful of almost everything about Diony-

sus, including his hair, which he calls "dainty tresses" such as a
woman might adorn herself with:

> Men say a stranger to the land hath come,
> A juggling sorcerer from Lydia-land,
> With essenced hair in gold tresses tossed,
> Wine-flushed, Love's witching graces in his eyes,
> Who with damsels day and night consorts,
> Making pretence of Evian mysteries.
> If I within these walls but prison him,
> Farewell to thyrsus-taboring, and to locks
> Free-tossed; for neck from shoulders will I hew
> (Euripides 1979a, 233–9)

Wise old Tiresias, however, recognizes the splendor and authen-
ticity of the new god, and welcomes him. He especially notes the
two great gifts of wine and sleep that Dionysus has given to
humankind. Tiresias and Cadmus honor Dionysus, and don-
ning fawnskin garb they join the maenad women in the god's
dancing procession.

When Pentheus sees these old men participating in the
riotous march, he mocks them:

> But lo, another marvel this—the seer
> Tiresias in dappled fawnskins clad!
> . . . A sight for laughter! (248–51)

Tiresias, however, is undaunted and replies to the king:

> I, then, and Cadmus whom thou laugh'st to scorn,
> Will wreathe our heads with ivy, and will dance—
> A greybeard pair, yet cannot we but dance. (322–4)

It soon becomes clear that Dionysus has a special call to the
women, and that he is leading them away from their sedate
domestic duties so that through him they might experience a
new freedom. Pentheus's anger at Dionysus for this seeming
seduction of the women of the realm grows; he especially com-
plains that Dionysus "drives women frenzied from the home"
(652). Rightly, Pentheus fears that he is losing control, for filled
with the spirit of the god, the women experience a new freedom;

they abandon themselves gloriously to instinct. Intoxicated with the god, they follow him into the wilds, leaving behind the sober domestic life and confinements to which Pentheus had subjected them.

The contrast between Dionysus's attitude toward the women and that of the patriarchal Pentheus is sharply drawn in Euripides' play: while Pentheus distrusts the women and would regulate their lives and loves, Dionysus trusts them to express their sexuality and love in their own way:

> Dionysus upon women will not thrust
> Chastity: in true womanhood inborn
> Dwells temperance touching all things evermore.
> This thou must heed; for in Bacchus' rites
> The virtuous-hearted shall not be undone. (315–8)

It is in the nature of the patriarchy for men to project their own sexual wantonness onto women and enforce on them a sexually restricted life better chosen for themselves. Dionysus, however, does not see the sexual energy of women as wanton; rather he sees it as regulated by their inmost and deepest selves. He does not fear an attitude of *panourgos* (anything goes) on the part of the women because he believes that women, in being true to love, are true to their own best nature.

Inevitably, the tension between Dionysus and Pentheus erupts into open conflict. Pentheus sends soldiers to capture Dionysus; they bind him securely and throw him into prison. But Dionysus easily frees himself from his bonds and brings about an earthquake which destroys both the prison and the palace of Pentheus as well. Meanwhile, the soldiers whom Pentheus had sent to bring the women back to their homes and "respectability" are easily routed because the women are magically defended against the soldiers' weapons. When Pentheus persists in the conflict, Dionysus casts a spell on him, and in his bewitched state Pentheus is obsessed with the desire to spy, to gaze on the women in their maenad revelry. Dionysus now feigns to be the friend of the befuddled Pentheus. He helps him fulfill his desire to gaze upon the women by dressing him in women's dress, but when the women discover the lecherous and spying king, they pursue him relentlessly, and when they catch him, they tear him to pieces with their own hands. Pentheus's mother, now a maenad herself, is the last to attack; seeing his impending doom, Pentheus begs for mercy and laments his fate:

> Tis I, O mother! thine own son
> Pentheus—thou bar'st me in Echion's hall!
> Have mercy, O my mother! for my sin.
> Murder not thy son—thy very son!
> (Euripides 1979a, 1118–21)

Heedless of her son's pleas, Pentheus's mother falls on him ferociously; she tears off her son's head and triumphantly bears it away. Thus was completed the triumph of Dionysus, friend to women, god of life and soul, over Pentheus, patriarchal adversary of all that the god held dear.

How are we to understand the meaning of this "strangest of all the gods"? The key element lies in his madness, but we must remember that this is not the common madness we know as insanity. Instead, it is the divine madness the Greeks called *mania*. We experience this *mania* when we are filled with the spirit of a god, that is, filled with a power and inspiration which do not come from the ego, nor from the common mentality, but from that supra-personal realm of the gods. From this realm true creativity—and sometimes destructiveness as well—emerges. As Plato made clear, the deepest inspiration a mortal can experience, in fact the source of all great inspiration, comes from "mania," not understood as the derangement of a sick mind, nor as possession by reckless effects, but as divine inspiration, which comes from that "indwelling" power that humankind has always called divinity. Neither is this mania a power and inspiration that a person can produce for himself or herself, or one that can be engendered through a drug; it can only come by the will of the divine. As Plato put it, "In reality the greatest blessings come to us through madness, *when it is sent as a gift of the gods*" (Plato 1984d, 224A7–9; emphasis mine). From this divine madness comes the inspiration of the poet, the inventor, the musician; indeed, it is the source not only of our particular genius, but of the genius of life itself.

It may be this divine madness which is symbolized in the

long hair and flowing locks of the god, an aspect of Dionysus to which Euripides especially called attention. It is interesting in this connection to note the emphasis on hair, especially long hair, in our so-called counter-culture. Our performers, musicians, and many other celebrities appear now in long hair, and we often emulate them. This style may well parallel "the long locks of hair" of Dionysus and express the soul's yearning for identification with the god.

All of this may bring with it an element of foolishness, but divine foolishness is also part of the Dionysian experience. It is interesting and important that when the old men Tiresias and Cadmus joined the entourage of Dionysus, they were castigated by Pentheus for their foolishness. We are used to thinking that old people should be dignified, and perhaps even solemn, but it may be that the proper way to live in old age is to identify not with the Wise Old Man but with the Fool. This point is well made by Zurich analyst Adolf Guggenbühl-Craig, who pointed out that an old man (or woman) who identified with the Wise Old Man would become autocratic and rigid, but if he lives with the archetype of the Fool as his companion, then he would remain alive and warmly human, imbued with what we may call the strange wisdom of Dionysus.

This divine madness is the secret of the "mystery" (*mustērion*) of the god. The *mustērion* of Dionysus, which like any *mustērion* is an experience of power into which a person must be initiated, brought a "new spiritual impulse" to the religion of Greece and, consequently, to the spirituality of the Western world. The old religion before Dionysus came, Jane Harrison notes, was a *do et dus*: "I do, and you do." That is, a human being does something for the god, like making a sacrifice, and the god does something for the human being in return (Harrison 1950). The new spirit of Dionysus, however, transcends this narrow and archaic understanding of the religious impulse. It is not a matter of doing something to please, placate, or cajole a deity so that the deity will do what we want; rather, it is a matter of experiencing that deity within oneself.

This was the new development in Greek religion which Dionysus brought. It also brought a new understanding of the means by which the soul was purified. A chief function of religion generally is to free or purge the soul from sin. Sin can come about either through breaking a divine law or commandment or through contamination or possession by evil. The former kind of sin calls for confession and restitution, but the latter state of sin calls for purification. Soldiers coming back from war, for instance, were regarded in many cultures as impure because they had shed blood; therefore, they had to undergo purification rites before being allowed back into the human community. This was both for the welfare of society and for the benefit of the soldiers who had engaged in the killing. Unfortunately, this wise psychology is overlooked in our supposedly enlightened culture, and no doubt the lack of a ritual of purification severely impaired the functioning of many returning Vietnam veterans. The new religion of Dionysus purified the soul from contamination. This it did not only by purging the soul of evil but also by infusing the soul with divinity, for a soul filled with divinity has no room in it for evil.

One way, therefore, of describing and understanding the Dionysian experience is to think of it as an intimate experience with an indwelling divine power, but at the same time this experience can be described as a "getting out of oneself," that is, an ecstasy in the original sense of the Greek word *ekstasis*, which means "to stand outside of one's [usual] self." To be filled with the god, therefore, is to be outside of that ordinary self of limited consciousness and dulled awareness and to step into a self we did not previously know existed, a self pulsating with energy and inspiration, a self we now experience as our own but which has its source in a power beyond the ego. The soul experiences this self as transcendent and creative; from this energy emerges inspiration, be it in art, music, science, or love.

Dionysus and Apollo are often contrasted by students of Greek mythology. Apollo is the deity of order, reason, clarity, and form. Dionysus, on the other hand, breaks down existing forms in order to generate creativity and enthusiasm in the original sense of that word which, as we have seen, means "to be filled with a god." Many commentators on Dionysus, ranging from modern commentators such as Jung and Nietzsche to ancient commentators dating back at least as far as Plutarch, have pointed out the contrast between Dionysus and Apollo (Plutarch 1970). Often, the contrast between the two is viewed as an enmity, the principle of one being an enemy to the principle of the other. This is the case when one opposite tries to exclude the other; on the other hand, the complete personality will allow both forms of energy to exist, albeit in a balance which can be maintained by a developed consciousness.

Interestingly, the well-known Greek maxim "know thyself," which has often been repeated in Christian and other religious traditions, relies on self-knowledge from both the Apollonian and the Dionysian sources. Whenever the ego stands apart and looks objectively at itself, it partakes of the Apollonian spirit; a great deal of the process of psychotherapy uses this Apollonian spirit to gain insight; we look at ourselves objectively to see the truth about who we are. At the same time, certain deep elements of the psyche can only be known through ecstasy, through experiences in which the ego, paradoxically, "loses" its usual self in order to know its deeper Self.

In Dionysian ecstasy the core of the creative is released. This can, however, be a dangerous experience, because where the creative emerges, the old existing order must first be torn down. If a person who is still caught in his or her egocentricity tries to possess this process, then the Dionysian energy can become perverted into a negative rather than inspired destruction of psychic order. It is possible, therefore, to overvalue the Dionysian energy, to forget that it lives best when related to its Apollonian opposite, just as the Apollonian order works best when it has the Dionysian as its companion. Professor Otto expressed this point nicely when he said of the emergence of the Dionysian energy:

> Greeted with wild shouts of joy, the form in which the truth appears is the frenzied, the all-engulfing torrent of life which wells up from the depths which gave it birth. In the myth [of Dionysus] and in the experience of those who have been affected by this event, the appearance of Dionysus brings with it nourishing intoxicating waters that bubble up from the earth. Rocks split open, and streams of water gush forth. Everything that has been locked up is released. The alien and the hostile unite in marvellous harmony. Age-old laws have suddenly lost their power, and even the dimensions of space and time are no longer valid. (Otto 1981, 95)

The important thing to note here is that what arrives with Dionysian energy is not an indulgence of the ego in wanton effects and destructiveness, but the *truth*: a truth so profound it cannot be grasped by the intellect, but can be known by the living spirit; a truth in which opposition is not created but dissolved in an ecstatic union in which that which has been erroneously suppressed is released, and the human spirit is free at last to be its truest self.

It remains to ponder the meaning of Dionysus today. First we must note that the Dionysian experience is that part of the individuation process in which fixed and rigid ego structures are dissolved, permitting the emergence of new energies from the Self. As Edward Edinger has pointed out, this aspect of the Dionysian experience partakes of the nature of the alchemical *solutio* (Edinger 1985, 60). The *solutio* refers to that stage in the alchemical process which transforms the base elements of the *prima materia* into the prized philosopher's stone (i.e., the Self); it is a process in which fixed, rigid elements are dissolved so they may be regrouped in a new, more vital way. As Jung and others have shown, the processes of alchemical change are symbolic of the individuation process. There comes a certain stage in our psychic development when the personality has become too fixed, too rigid, too dominated by the ego and the rational; then it is essential that a *solutio* take place, that the Self can emerge and replace the too fixed and rigid ego as the center of the personality.

The Dionysian can also be seen as the antidote to what can be called the "loneliness of the ego." Our culture strives to build up an independent autonomous ego, an ego at home in the world of separation, an ego which has power and which can compete and "make it to the top." Such an ego development has much to commend it, but it can go too far. When it does, then a longing for the opposite begins: a longing for union, not separation; for ecstasy, not reason; for surrender to life, not power; for inspiration, not control. It is a longing to escape from our egos, which live on their lonely island, and instead merge into oneness with other people, with life, with cosmos, even with God, for the human soul cannot stand alone forever.[3]

This longing to escape from our lonely ego-islands can become so great that many of us unwittingly exchange our individual identity for a group identity. Now we are no longer alone! Now we feel ourselves part of the larger whole! But this kind of group identification, which Jung termed *participation mystique,* is not the Dionysian answer, for participation mystique leads to a negative extinction of individual consciousness through its submergence in a group consciousness. The Dionysian experience leads to a heightened consciousness. The true Dionysian experience is not the extinction of the ego as such, but the merging of the ego with a divinity beyond itself, a divinity which evokes both religious awe and humanity, and engenders a heightened awareness. Thus, the Dionysian experience is not to be confused with lawlessness, nor simply to be thought of as the abandonment of reason and restraint. The emphasis should not be on what seems abandoned, but on what is added to consciousness. Salvation is not achieved by rejecting one side of a pair of opposites, but is found by experiencing their creative union.

It cannot be said too often that there is no independent freedom for the ego. The ego must always relate itself to something. If the ego divests itself of all sense of awe and allegiance to divinity, it does not then become free—for it will serve some devil instead. In fact, the ego itself becomes a devil as soon as it sets itself up as the Center. This is why Fritz Kunkel once said, "The secret is, the ego is the devil."[4] Whenever the ego tries to stand alone, the soul is abandoned; and where the soul is empty, evil comes to fill it. The power of evil is too strong for the empty soul to withstand. Jung put it well when he wrote to William W., one of the founders of Alcoholics Anonymous, that letter alluded to in chapter 4. As he there remarked: "the evil principle . . . leads the unrecognized spiritual need into perdition, if it is not counter-acted" (1953b, 624).

Dionysus comes as the liberator of the soul because he frees that which has been repressed and fills the empty soul with his power. That women especially were his devotees suggests that the imprisoned element was, and still is, the feminine. Wherever the feminine is freed from its constraints to be truly itself, whether this liberation takes place in a man or a woman, then the Dionysian element can be present. This liberation of the feminine, however, is not to be confused with contemporary feminism as such, worthy though the social goals of feminism may be. The primary emphasis of the Dionysian experience is not to achieve social change, but to release all that is wild and free in the human soul.

This liberation of the feminine in the soul, however, is not achieved through the rejection of the *logos*, the powers of the masculine. What we see in the Dionysian liberation is not the victory of one element over another, but a release of all that belongs to the soul, so that the soul's various elements may unite. This union may be aided by clear Apollonian insight, but ultimately the union is made from the depths—through religious experience, if you like. Walter Otto once said of this mysterious union of the soul: "No arbitrary concept reconciles them. It is only in the absence of all agreement, in supreme tension, when the antitheses become wild and infinite, that the great mystery of oneness is proclaimed from the very depths of being" (1981, 120).

Dionysian energy teems with life, yet it also embraces death. This idea may appear strange to us, since in our culture death is seen as the enemy and life is valued above all things. Yet, in the ultimate mystery of Dionysus, life and death are never far apart, and the flowering of life is never far from its ecstatic extinction in death. The one who wants to live fully must also accept death. Only when the ego can surrender to this reality can it experience the true *ekstasis*, for only then can it truly surrender itself.

The soul still hungers for the Dionysian experience, but we no longer know how to find it. Having killed the irrational in our culture, we have difficulty in finding creative ecstasy. Having denied the reality of the soul, with its penchant for all that is irrational in the best sense of that word, we are hardly in a position to fulfill her needs. Nevertheless, needs are there, and the needs of the soul are our deepest needs. We hunger to escape from the prison of rationality, conformity, mediocrity, and taking more and more power to the ego. This unfulfilled and often unrecognized longing in us for the freedom of the Dionysian experience is certainly one of the important factors in drug addiction. The longing of the soul for creative dissolution in the god of ecstasy can be a major factor in the insatiable craving of the alcoholic for drink; in alcohol is offered promise, however false it may be, of a solution in which rigid ego structures are dissolved through a Dionysian experience. But, alas! the god does not come through a drug, nor through common drunkenness!

111

The Dionysian experience we see exemplified in ancient literature describes an experience filled with overflowing vitality of life. Our contemporary culture appears to attempt to duplicate the Dionysian experience through excitement, but the experience of true Dionysian excitement eludes us because our attempt is based largely on a desire to excite the ego, rather than toward leading the ego to participate in the natural flow of life that comes from soul. Soulless excitement may lead to a temporary "high," but not to the ego-transcending experience of the god of ecstasy. In the ancient cult, devotees of Dionysus surrendered themselves to the experience of a divinity. In our culture, having killed the gods, we are left with an unconscious, unsatisfied longing for ecstasy that leads us to strive for more and more excitement to arouse us from outside of ourselves. We have apparently become addicted to excitement precisely because we have lost touch with those powers within us which could bring true ecstasy.

Lacking a sense of the divine, we naturally cannot find the divinity within ourselves; having "killed the gods" we are left with the boredom and emptiness of the egocentric ego. As a consequence, most of our television programs and other forms of mass entertainment turn to an artificially contrived excitement, fed to us from outside instead of being discovered within. One problem with this kind of excitement is that to maintain the desired level of outer stimulation, we have to keep "turning up the volume" lest we sink back into our emptiness. Many of our television programs, perhaps most of our televised athletic events with the ever-excited voices of the announcers, and even many of our newscasters with their ever more strident voices and obsession with the most bizarre element in our national life, give evidence that we find ourselves bored and have become addicted to infusions of excitement from outside ourselves to assuage our emptiness within. The dosage, as with any addiction, must always be increased to continue to render the desired effect. Thus, "the volume must always be turned up more" to maintain the sense of excitement.

Our difficulty today in finding true ecstasy, and our substitution of excitement instead, may also influence our criminal element. Asked what may have caused the increase in crime in our country, one lifelong prison chaplain said, "I don't know, except for one thing. These people who are criminals are addicted to excitement."[5] So addicted, who would be satisfied with a nine-to-five job when a bank could be robbed instead?

It is not excitement in itself that brings us to the ecstatic experience. People in ancient times did not use excitement to find god; they found the god first and then were filled with the soul-fulfilling ecstatic energy of the Dionysian spirit. Artificial ways of finding excitement lead to less, not more, consciousness, whereas the true Dionysian spirit heightens our spiritual awareness. Neither can we try to find the true Dionysian spirit by contriving quasi-religious rituals, for rituals lack energy when they are performed for their own sake instead of for the sake of a divinity. If we have killed our sense of the divine, our awareness of what is holy, our ability to be struck with awe and to subordinate our egos to a greater power, then disembodied rituals performed only in the service of the ego cannot save us.

It remains only to compare Dionysus with Christ. To anyone who has been a participant in a contemporary staid Christian church, it may seem strange to compare Christ with Dionysus, but the comparisons are striking. To begin with, Christ, like Dionysus, is the god of freedom (an expression once used by C. G. Jung); he does not represent the wanton freedom of "anything goes," but the true freedom which comes when the ego serves the creative center. Like Dionysus, Christ also expressed the essence of life, but was destined to die that the life he expressed might be mystically made available to all. Like Dionysus, Christ was also the god for the feminine and for women, a revolutionary figure as far as the rights of the feminine were concerned, in an otherwise starkly masculine culture.[6] Both Christ and Dionysus are associated with the vine, with the serpent, and especially with the Eucharistic wine which frees the soul from bondage to sin and the Law, and liberates the soul to the freedom of Christ.[7]

Notes

1. *Mustērion*—something which can be known only through initiation or intimate personal experience.

113

2. From the works of the 5th century A.D. poet Nonnus, author of a Greek epic about Dionysus and his many adventures.
3. For insight into the need of the soul for oneness with others, see John 17, and my commentary in *Mystical Christianity* (Sanford 1993).
4. An oft-quoted statement by Fritz Kunkel, author of *Creation Continues* and many other books. See Sanford 1984.
5. My thanks to Chaplain Glenn S. Crook for this insight.
6. See Sanford 1993, ch. 5.
7. Cf. John 15:1–16:5 and Sanford 1993, ch. 26. Cf. John 3:14 and Sanford 1993, ch. 2. Cf. Sanford 1993, ch. 15.

Works Cited

Aeschylus. 1983a. 1926. *Agamemnon*. Trans. H. Weir Smyth. Loeb Classical Library Edition. Cambridge, Mass.: Harvard University Press.

_____. 1983b. 1926. *Eumenides*. Trans. H. Weir Smyth. Loeb Classical Library Edition. Cambridge, Mass.: Harvard University Press.

_____. 1988. 1922. *Prometheus Bound*. Trans. H. Weir Smyth. Loeb Classical Library Edition. Cambridge, Mass.: Harvard University Press.

Augustine. 1978. 1963. *City of God*. Trans. William M. Green. Loeb Classical Library Edition. Vol. 2. Cambridge, Mass.: Harvard University Press.

Aoki, Haruo. 1979. Nez Percé texts. *University of California Publications in Linguistics*. Vol. 90. Berkeley: University of California Press.

Broster, Joan A. 1981. *Amaghirha: Religion, magic and medicine in Transkei*. Johannesburg: Via Africa Limited.

Classic Greek Dictionary. 1901. New York: Hinds & Noble.

Cowan, Lynn. 1982. *Masochism: A Jungian view*. Dallas: Spring Publications.

Dodds, E. R. 1957. *The Greeks and the irrational*. Boston: Beacon Press.

Edinger, Edward F. 1985. *Anatomy of the psyche*. La Salle, Ill.: Open Court Press.

Edmunds, L. 1990. *Approaches to Greek mythology*. Baltimore and London: Johns Hopkins University Press.

Euripides. 1979a. 1912. *The Bacchanals*. Trans. Arthur S. Way. In *Euripides*. Loeb Classical Library Edition. Vol. 3. Cambridge, Mass.: Harvard University Press.

_____. 1979b. 1912. *Hippolytus*. Trans. Arthur S. Way. In *Euripides*. Loeb Classical Library Edition. Vol. 4. Cambridge, Mass.: Harvard University Press.

_____. 1979c. 1912. *Medea*. Trans. Arthur S. Way. In *Euripides*. Loeb Classical Library Edition. Vol. 4. Cambridge, Mass.: Harvard University Press.

Harrison, Jane. 1955. *Prologomena to the study of Greek religion*. New York: Meridian Books, Inc.

Herodotus. 1990. 1920. *The History*. In 4 vols. Trans. A. D. Godley. Loeb Classical Library Edition. Cambridge, Mass.: Harvard University Press.

Hesiod. 1982a. 1914. *Homeric hymn to Aphrodite*. Trans. Hugh G. Evelyn-White. Loeb Classical Library Edition. Cambridge, Mass.: Harvard University Press.

_____. 1982b. 1914. *Works and days*. Trans. Hugh G. Evelyn-White. Loeb Classical Library Edition. Cambridge, Mass.: Harvard University Press.

Homer. 1978. 1924. *The Iliad*. 2 vols. Trans. A. T. Murray. Loeb Classical Library Edition. Cambridge, Mass.: Harvard University Press.

_____. 1984. 1919. *The Odyssey*. 2 vols. Trans. A. T. Murray. Loeb Classical Library Edition. Cambridge, Mass.: Harvard University Press.

Jung, C. G. 1953a. The archetypes of the collective unconscious. *Collected Works*. Vol. 7. New York: Pantheon Books.

_____. 1953b. *Letters*. Vol. 2. Princeton, N. J.: Princeton University Press.

Kerényi, C. 1951. *The gods of the Greeks*. Trans. Norman Cameron. London: Thames & Hudson.

Lucretius. 1992. 1924. *On the nature of things*. Trans. W. H. D. Rouse. Loeb Classical Library Edition. Cambridge, Mass.: Harvard University Press.

Martyr, Justin. 1957. *First apology*. In *The Ante-Nicene Fathers*. Vol. 1. Grand Rapids, Mich.: Wm. B. Eerdmans Publishing Co. 159–87.

Methodius. 1957. *Banquet of the ten virgins*. In *The Ante-Nicene Fathers*. Vol. 6. Grand Rapids, Mich.: Wm. B. Eerdmans Publishing Co. 309–355.

Origen. 1957. *De Principiis*. In *The Ante-Nicene Fathers*. Vol. 4. Grand Rapids, Mich.: Wm. B. Eerdmans Publishing Co. 239–384.

Otto, Walter. 1981. *Dionysus: Myth and cult*. Dallas: Spring Publications.

Plato. 1984a. 1926. *Apology*. Trans. W. R. M. Lamb. In *Plato*. Vol. 1. Loeb Classical Library Edition. Cambridge, Mass.: Harvard University Press.

_____. 1984b. 1926. *Leges*. Trans. R. G. Bury. In *Plato*. Vols. 6–7. Loeb Classical Library Edition. Cambridge, Mass.: Harvard University Press.

_____. 1984c. 1926. *Phaedo*. Trans. W. R. M. Lamb. In *Plato*. Vol. 1. Loeb Classical Library Edition. Cambridge, Mass.: Harvard University Press.

_____. 1984d. 1926. *Phraedrus*. Trans. W. R. M. Lamb. In *Plato*. Vol. 1. Loeb Classical Library Edition. Cambridge, Mass.: Harvard University Press.

_____. 1984e. 1926. *Symposium*. Trans. W. R. M. Lamb. In *Plato*. Vol. 3. Loeb Classical Library Edition. Cambridge, Mass.: Harvard University Press.

Plutarch. 1962. *Antony*. In *Plutarch's lives*. Modern Library Edition. Trans. John Dryden. Rev. Arthur Hugh Clough. New York: Random House. 1105–52.

_____. 1970. *Plutarch's de Iside et Osiride*. Translation of "Peri Isidos kai Osiridos" from the *Moralia*. Trans. J. Gwyn Griffiths. Cardiff: University of Wales, 1970.

Roberts, Alexander, and James A. Donaldson. 1885–96. *The Ante-nicene fathers: the writings of the fathers down to A. D. 325*. 10 vols. Rev. A. Cleveland Coxe. Buffalo: Christian Literature Publishing Co. Repr. 1957. Grand Rapids, Mich.: Wm. B. Eerdmans Publishing Co.

Sanford, John A. 1974. *The man who wrestled with God*. Medwah, N. J.: Paulist Press.

_____. 1987. *The kingdom within: The inner meaning of the sayings of Jesus*. San Francisco: HarperCollins.

_____. 1992. *Healing body and soul*. Louisville, Kty.: Westminster/John Knox Press.

_____. 1993. *Mystical Christianity*. New York: Crossroad/Continuum Pub. Co.

_____., ed. 1984. *Fritz Kunkel: Selected writings*. Medwah, N. J.: Paulist Press.

Sophocles. 1962. *Antigone*. Trans. F. Storr. In *Sophocles*. Vol. 2. Loeb Classical Library Edition. Cambridge, Mass.: Harvard University Press.

Tertullian. 1957. *Treatise on the soul* (181–235) and *Against Marcion* (269–476). Trans. Peter Holmes. In *The Ante-Nicene Fathers*. Vol. 3. Grand Rapids, Mich.: Wm. B. Eerdmans Publishing Co.

Tuchman, Barbara. 1948. *The march of folly*. New York: Ballantine.

Upton, Charles. 1993. *Hammering hot iron: A spiritual critique of Bly's Iron John*. Wheaton, Ill.: Quest Books/Theosophical Publishing House.

Wilhelm, Richard, trans. 1950. *I Ching*. Vol. 2. Bollingen Series XIX. New York: Bollingen Foundation, Inc., and Pantheon Books.

Zabriskie, Philip. 1974. Goddesses in our midst. *Quadrant Magazine* (Fall).

INDEX